EMBRACED
BY THE
SPIRIT

Stay blessed!

Paul Collins

PAUL COLLINS

EMBRACED BY THE SPIRIT
Copyright © 2005 by Paul Collins

ISBN: 0-9755311-8-2

Published by

LifeBridge
Books
P.O. BOX 49428
CHARLOTTE, NC 28277

Printed in the United States of America.

DEDICATION

This book is dedicated to West Park United Methodist Church in my hometown of Moberly, Missouri. They were the first to encourage me regarding ministry. Most of those wonderful "people called Methodists" of my childhood are now in heaven, but they are alive in my memory. I also acknowledge the members and friends of churches where I served as pastor. They provided me with valuable experiences and many opportunities to grow in my relationship with the Holy Spirit.

CONTENTS

INTRODUCTION

What you are about to read is the result of an unexpected journey—one I certainly did not plan, but a spiritual adventure for which I will forever be grateful.

As you will learn in this book, I like to pray before getting out of bed in the morning. For years, my daily habit had been to thank God for everything good: past, present, and future. I would inevitably follow this with a laundry list of requests—often cloaked in more thanks for blessings yet to come.

One morning, I was stopped in my mental tracks. The Holy Spirit began telling me to stop thinking "thoughts" and simply allow Him to embrace me. He also added, "In order for Me to embrace you, I need you to reach out and embrace me."

The message was crystal clear: a hug works two ways—it's not enough when practiced by just one of the parties.

I remember the times I would hug someone who was as cold as a marble statue. Oh, the person didn't mean to be impersonal or aloof, sadly, the individual just did not know how to respond or show affection.

Often, people react like small children who are

timid. After a hug, their shyness causes them to show their appreciation with nothing more than a smile.

The Holy Spirit wants much more from us—He desires to be embraced.

UNLIMITED OPTIONS

Some of what we experience in our Christian walk can require a search of the scriptures for justification. We don't always have advance notice regarding the ways God will use for us to hear His voice. We talk about hearing Him in the sounds of nature, the sights of the universe, and the love of others toward us. However, when God moves away from these traditional methodologies, He delights us with His unlimited options.

The Lord can bless us, speak to us, and hear us in circumstances we haven't even imagined. As the Bible informs, He, *"...by the power at work within us is able to accomplish abundantly far more than all we can ask or imagine"* (Ephesians 3:20).

It is difficult to explain my delight when I was invited to embrace the Holy Spirit? I joyfully forfeited my litany of requests. I didn't need *anything* because I was entering a special time of fellowship with my Lord. After all, when the Holy Spirit is present, Jesus and the Father are also there. As someone who believes in the Trinity—God the Father, God the Son and God the Holy Spirit—I have learned that to hear the voice of *one* is to hear the voice of *all three*.

Since the time Jesus died, rose from the tomb and ascended to the Father, the Holy Spirit has been available to us on an intense, yet gentle, personal basis. He was there at creation, as the Spirit of God moved over the deep darkness. He descended on Jesus at His baptism by John, and was breathed on the ten disciples by Jesus following His resurrection (Judas was dead and Thomas was missing).

"WHY NOT?"

As you receive the message written on these pages, you may ask, "Can I have such an experience with the Holy Spirit?"

A better question might be, "Why not?"

I know of no reason for you to be shunned if you are born again and led by the Spirit. Paul the Apostle wrote these words to the Christians at Rome: *"For all who are led by the Spirit of God are children of God"* (Romans 8:14).

The moment you confessed your faith in Christ, you became a child of God. As such, the Holy Spirit is walking with you whether or not you know or sense His presence.

Just as the Holy Spirit knew me before I knew Him, be assured He knows and is with you even when your mind is far-removed from the reality of God's continual love. Once you accept this truth, it becomes much easier to practice the concept of "praying without ceasing." These words of Paul have been difficult for Christians to comprehend until they learn how to experience the enveloping, surrounding love of the Spirit.

Scripture tells us, *"...it is that very Spirit bearing witness with our spirit that we are children of God"* (Romans 8:16).

These verses from Romans 8 reveal an over-looked truth: Christians, like children, live in a family. That is, we are members of a community—the Body of Christ on earth.

This speaks to our mutually dependent situation. We will hear God better, see His evidence more clearly, and experience His embrace more fully when we have an active engagement with others who are like-minded.

WEEKLY ENCOUNTERS

The teachings in this book were primarily written during a period of over two years when I spent every Wednesday alone in my study—reading the Word, praying and learning to hear the voice of the Holy Spirit.

I must admit, the experience of these weekly encounters became almost like an addiction. I would go into my study and become more and more reluctant to leave—craving just one more word from God.

The most pointed, yet uplifting, message I ever received in those days was when the Lord finally said to me, "Paul, I can speak to you on days other than Wednesdays!"

Immediately, I knew the retreats (as a regular, weekly event) were over. I was made aware that I had the great privilege to listen for His voice *every* day, in *all* circumstances, and in *any* surroundings. I realized the Holy Spirit can speak in the midst of the noise and bustle of this world. He can be heard by the human heart, spirit, and mind even if there are a thousand other voices vying for attention. I came to the place where my heart's cry was, "More of you, Lord" and "Holy Spirit you are welcome."

Today, it is my prayer that as the result of reading this book you will also say, "Embrace me, Holy Spirit."

– Paul Collins

CHAPTER 1

AN UNEXPECTED CALL

You won't find many ministers who were called to preach even before they were converted, yet that is exactly what happened to me.

At the tender age of nine, in a little Methodist church in my hometown of Moberly, Missouri, as clear as anything I had ever heard, the Lord planted these words in my heart: "You are going to be a minister of the Gospel."

I felt this was such a private matter I didn't tell my parents—or any of my friends. It was a secret just between the Lord and me.

I knew what God said to me was true, but I tucked it into the back of my mind and continued to be a small town kid.

However, the major turning point in my life didn't occur until ten years later. At the age of 19, in January, 1955, I accepted Christ as my personal Savior and became a born again believer. Only then did I *accept* God's earlier call on my life.

THE "CARAVAN"

It was blustery and cold in Moberly, yet my heart was on fire with the zeal of one who had finally found his purpose and reason for being. At the time I had already started my college studies as a pre-med student.

Very few friends and family understood my call to ministry—except for some faithful "little old ladies" in our church. They had been praying for me for years, and instructing me in the Bible and matters of faith.

Almost immediately, I was invited to join a group of teens calling themselves "The Gospel Youth Caravan" that held Friday night meetings and other gatherings in the area.

I can still remember being asked to preach my first sermon at one of the Caravan services—with several of my high school and college classmates in the audience. I was challenged, but not intimidated, since I knew this was God's plan for my life.

After that evening, I was the speaker every other Friday night at the youth outreach. Even though I was a member of the Methodist Church, I began preaching without a denominational banner.

ME? A PASTOR?

During these life-altering days, I changed my college major from pre-med to pre-theological and was more than excited about the future.

By the time I reached my junior year, I was asked by my denomination to become the pastor of a Methodist church, one of three I would lead while I graduated from college and began my seminary studies.

My first assignment was the church in Clifton Hill, Missouri, a small community of about 250 located just 13 miles west of my hometown of Moberly.

I can still see the attractive brick church located on a main corner of town. It was quite an adventure for a barely 20-year-old student at Central Methodist College (now a University). The school was

I STILL CHUCKLE AT HOW I CONSIDERED MYSELF AN ACCOMPLISHED PREACHER IN THOSE EARLY DAYS.

33 miles away in Fayette. I commuted to college every morning and drove to Moberly, another 15 miles away, in the afternoon to work as a meat cutter to make ends meet. I still chuckle at how I considered myself an

accomplished preacher in those early days. Little did I know!

An Exercise in Public Relations

The next church I pastored was in Huntsville, six miles closer to Moberly, paid twice the salary (Wow! I was now receiving $3,200 a year), and had a much nicer parsonage. It was a county seat town of about 1500 people.

My experience in the county seat town was an exercise in public relations rather than power. No matter what I said, people just didn't respond to an altar call. Looking back, I failed to give them a valid reason to come forward—never offering to pray for their salvation, healing or deliverance.

In those three Huntsville years, I developed into the town's premier preacher of funerals. I would have rather been known as one who knew the Holy Spirit.

In the process of pastoring I became married and we had two small children (another would arrive later). I also was ordained as a minster in the United Methodist Church—and remain so until this day.

The "Kid Parson"

When I think of the early success I experienced in ministry, I realize it was mostly a case of style over substance. Yes, I could preach with persuasion, teach the Word and counsel those with personal problems.

People were very complimentary and had flattering things to say. Even when I grew a little older and could no longer be considered a "kid parson," the accolades continued.

As I look back, the performance they praised was shallow because I had passion but no power. I spoke *about* the Holy Spirit, but He was not real to me.

The wonderful people who blessed my life in so many ways were being deprived of the deeper things of the Almighty because I knew practically nothing concerning the Spirit of God.

I SPOKE ABOUT THE HOLY SPIRIT, BUT HE WAS NOT REAL TO ME.

My time earning a college degree, completing seminary, and finishing a Doctor of Theology in Christian Psychology and The Bible, was not wasted. It gave me a strong foundation.

Even though ministry should be "call driven," there is a place for formal education. After all, the apostle Paul was an educated man and took another three years to prepare for Christian ministry.

WHO WOULD I COPY?

During the Gospel Youth Caravan days I aspired to be Billy Graham. In those years, I looked for role models. Later, when I watched the television

17

presentations of Oral Roberts under his big tent, I wasn't so sure about his "laying on of hands," but wanted to copy his oratorical style.

During my seminary experience, however, I fancied myself to be another apostle Paul—because I enjoyed his letters and was becoming more "educated."

In all my time of studying his writings, how could I have missed Paul's teachings on the Holy Spirit? In reality, no one should seriously aspire to be like the great apostle unless you know the Spirit and are willing to sacrifice. Looking back, I didn't satisfy either requirement.

HE KNEW ME BEFORE I KNEW HIM. HOW I MARVEL AT THE PATIENCE OF GOD.

Because I was willing and able to pursue a Methodist education, the denomination provided me with a church to pastor. Without knowing what was taking place, I was following a career path, yet the Holy Spirit was fulfilling my calling. He knew me before I knew Him. I marvel at the patience of God!

ONLY AN "INFLUENCE?"

I have far too many memories of standing behind the sacred desk spending God's precious time attempting to dynamically speak words to persuade my hearers to be regular in church attendance or to live by

18

biblical principles. Seldom did I mention the Holy Spirit.

To my shame, when I mentioned Him, I referred to the Spirit as "it." One message in particular stands out in my mind. In a sermon I preached to my congregation at Hyde Park Methodist Church in St. Joseph, Missouri, I was forcefully proclaiming the Holy Spirit to be God's influence. Over and over I made the comparison to the way we have sway over others even when we are miles apart. Never once did it cross my mind to tell the people that the Holy Spirit is the Third Person of the Trinity and, thus, He is God!

I served at Hyde Park from 1959 to 1964—a church filled with children, young married couples and middle-aged seasoned leaders. It buzzed with activity, hosting a long list of scouting organizations and groups for every segment of the congregation.

They tolerated my absence four days a week so I could commute to Kansas City to attend St. Paul School of Theology, a Methodist Seminary, for three of the five years I was there.

The Holy Spirit was active even though I must have been breaking His heart.

WHO WOULD BE CALLING?

It was August, 1963. I had just set down my suitcase at Howard Payne Hall, a dormitory on the campus of Central Methodist College in Fayette, and

19

was getting ready for the annual pastors' school.

When I heard the telephone ring in the hall, it didn't occur that someone would be calling for me! The old pay phone was a good match for the antique dorm.

Little did I know that picking up the receiver would open a new life and an unexpected kind of ministry. Yet, at the time, it was a window through which I failed to see the direction God was leading.

Years later I would understand.

The wood floors in the dorm were the originals, which made it impossible to walk anywhere without everyone within earshot knowing your whereabouts. I felt rather conspicuous and self-conscious with other ministers peeking out of their dorm doors to see who I was and, I imagined, curious as to why I would be receiving a phone call so soon after arriving at the annual pastors' school.

VIRGINIA'S STORY

The voice on the other end of the line sent shock waves through me. Virginia Shortle, one of the young, beautiful mothers in the Hyde Park church I was pastoring, had been diagnosed with cancer. There was a malignancy behind her right eye and it had to be removed the next day.

To complicate the matter, she was three months pregnant with her third child.

I was told only a local anesthetic could be

administered for fear of losing the baby. There was also the very likely possibility a tiny piece of the cancer would break away, enter the blood stream, and cause both mother and child to die in a matter of weeks.

My unpacked case, suit bag and briefcase were thrown into the trunk of my Chevrolet and I hurried back to St. Joe to be ready to follow Virginia's husband, Jerry, and her sister to the Kansas University Medical Center in the metropolitan Kansas City area.

We arrived early the next morning to minister to Virginia before the surgery.

When I saw her, I was unable to say anything profound, theological, or "pastorally correct." From somewhere I uttered these simple words: "Virginia, I don't know what to say. I just feel like I should read the 91st Psalm and then pray."

"VIRGINIA, I DON'T KNOW WHAT TO SAY. I JUST FEEL LIKE I SHOULD READ THE 91ST PSALM AND THEN PRAY."

That's exactly what I did. I opened my Bible and shared these words:

"He that dwelleth in the secret place of the most High shall abide under the shadow of the Almighty. I will say of the Lord, He is my refuge and my fortress: my God; in him will I trust.

Surely he shall deliver thee from the snare of the fowler, and from the noisome pestilence. He shall cover thee with his feathers, and under his wings shalt thou trust: his truth shall be thy shield and buckler" (Psalm 91:1-4 KJV).

And I concluded with the last two verses of the chapter:

"He shall call upon me, and I will answer him: I will be with him in trouble; I will deliver him, and honor him. With long life will I satisfy him, and show him my salvation" (vv.15-16).

As I finished reading, Virginia looked up and softly said, "Now I'm ready."

AS I FINISHED READING, VIRGINIA LOOKED UP AND SOFTLY SAID, "NOW, I'M READY."

The staff attendants were waiting to roll her into surgery.

Thirty minutes later, she was returned to her room —minus her right eye but in great spirits and very encouraged. Neither she, nor any of us, knew that the doctors believed she would only live a matter of weeks in spite of the surgery.

A BABY'S CRY

A few months later, her husband Jerry called me to join him at St. Francis Hospital in St. Joe. We walked the hall together outside the delivery room until the baby's cry stopped us in our tracks. Jerry and Virginia were now the proud parents of three children. What a miracle! The baby was healthy and so was her mother. Later, two more children would join the happy family.

There is more to this story, but the next installment did not occur for another 35 years. We will come back to her journey later.

Because of the healing touch which spared Virginia, the door to a new life and ministry had appeared and, at the time, I didn't know how to walk through it.

I had been preaching powerfully, energetically, and persuasively, yet I did not personally know the Holy Spirit—but, again, He certainly knew me!

I had always considered the Spirit to be God's *personality* or *influence,* never giving much thought to Him being the Third Person of the Trinity. And, because of my ecclesiastical upbringing, shied away from what the Bible teaches concerning healing and deliverance.

However, Virginia's miraculous touch from God caused me to delve into scripture as never before.

WHAT COULD HAVE BEEN!

During all of the time spent in a Methodist college

23

and seminary, I was never taught anything of substance concerning the Holy Spirit. Even in my upbringing in the church, it was a subject rarely discussed.

I have often pondered what *could have been* if I had only known the Holy Spirit in my early years of ministry. What if the spiritual gifts He later placed on my life had been in operation?

Yes, I preached Christ, and, in the life of Virginia, I witnessed a healing first-hand. Yet, I cannot help but wonder how many missed their miracle because I didn't truly know the Holy Spirit? How many fell by the wayside because I did not have the power of God actively engaged on the scene of my ministry? What could the church have been if I had known the reality of 1 Corinthians 12? How would it have impacted lives?

WHERE WERE THE WONDERS?

We cannot find fault with God. He says, *"My people are destroyed for lack of knowledge"* (Hosea 4:6).

How could I continually be so blind to the fact that before Jesus ascended to heaven, He declared signs and wonders would follow the preaching of the Word. He left His followers with this comand: *"Go into all the world and proclaim the good news to the whole creation. The one who believes and is baptized will be saved; but the one who does not believe will be condemned. And these signs will accompany those who believe: by using my name they will cast out demons; they will speak in new tongues...they will lay their hands on the sick, and they will recover"* (Mark 16:15-18).

Like countless others, I labored in the vineyard for years without the fruit of the Spirit at work. Where were the "signs?" Where were the "wonders?"

LIKE COUNTLESS OTHERS, I LABORED IN THE VINEYARD WITHOUT THE FRUIT OF THE SPIRIT AT WORK.

Ministry must be more than simply a career. The most unfulfilled days of my life were when I was climbing the ranks of a denomination, being promoted beyond my years into large churches. However, as I later told a friend, "I was a seminary graduate who didn't know beans!"

EARLY SIGNS

For nearly two decades in the ministry, the Spirit was slowly introducing Himself to me. Usually, I only recognized His presence in hindsight. At other times He became quite tangible.

On one occasion I was seated at the soda fountain of a Five and Dime store in Springfield, Missouri, with a fellow Methodist minister. We were discussing how God was working in our lives.

Quietly, so no one else could hear, I shared with my colleague a most unusual experience which had come upon me more than once. "Recently, when I have been in prayer," I told him, "I have felt a tingling sensation in my hands."

"What do you believe it means?" he asked.

"The only thing I can think of is that God is going to use me in some kind of healing ministry," I confided. "Perhaps, some day I will lay hands on the sick and they will be healed."

ONE NIGHT IN AUGUST

I didn't give this much more thought until the time finally came when my years of moving closer to the Holy Spirit reached a crescendo.

It was the first week of August, 1977. I was kneeling by the side of my bed, earnestly seeking the touch of the Holy Spirit. That night, I stood up and got into bed—but something urged me to continue talking with the Lord.

At that moment, the unthinkable happened to this Methodist. I began praying in a language I had never been taught. Suddenly, I experienced the physical *evidence* of the Holy Spirit.

I was both shocked and blessed beyond description—and as you will discover later in this book—my life would never be the same.

MY PRAYER FOR YOU
*I pray the Holy Spirit will make
Himself real to you today. He is near at
this very moment, waiting for you to welcome
His embrace. May your life be forever
changed by the reality of His presence.*

CHAPTER 2

A CHRONICLE OF THE SPIRIT

It was many years into my pulpit ministry when I began to earnestly study the Book of Acts and learned from Scripture who the Holy Spirit truly is.

Acts was written approximately 63 years after the death of our Lord Jesus Christ and its author, according to most Bible scholars, is Luke the physician.

The theme of the Acts of the Apostles is the triumphant spread of the Gospel. This was:

- Not through the power of man.
- Not through the power of an organization or bureaucracy.
- Not through the power of a college or seminary.

■ Not through the power of denominations —since there were none in existence at that time.

The Gospel expanded through the *power of the Holy Spirit.*

Acts chronicles the evangelization of the world surrounding the Mediterranean Sea during the first century A.D.

THE MISSION

One of the purposes of this revealing book was to show that the Gospel was taken from the narrow borders of Judaism into the Gentile world, which included everyone who wasn't a Jew. How the Gospel made this phenomenal transition into the rather wild world of the Gentiles, in spite of opposition and persecution, is itself a miraculous story.

Another purpose was to reveal the role of the Holy Spirit in the church. Its mission included emphasizing the Spirit as God's provision for empowering the believers to proclaim the Gospel and continue the ministry of Jesus.

Let me ask you to read that again so you will "inhale" the role of the Spirit in the church's mission—emphasizing the Holy Spirit as God's provider of His provision.

The Spirit continues the same mission today, giving

the church power to proclaim the Gospel and to continue the ministry of Jesus.

So it's quite evident this is not only the Book of the Acts of the Apostles, it is a chronicle of the Acts of the Holy Spirit.

It was this power working through these first generation Christians which enabled Christianity to break out of the narrow confines of Judaism and spread into the Gentile world. This same miraculous power continues to spread the message of Christ in our generation.

THIS IS NOT ONLY THE BOOK OF THE ACTS OF THE APOSTLES, IT IS A CHRONICLE OF THE ACTS OF THE HOLY SPIRIT.

The Book of Acts reveals that this empowerment took place because the Holy Spirit *baptized* people. It was not just so they could speak in tongues or say, "I've been baptized by the Holy Ghost." Rather, it was so they would be more effective and have the power to continue becoming better enabled to proclaim the Gospel.

A DIVINE EMPOWERMENT

First century Christians were fervent and intense in their efforts to win others as followers of Jesus the Nazarene. Why? Because the ministry of Christ had captured their hearts.

What was the ministry of Jesus? Acts 10:38 reports *"how God anointed Jesus of Nazareth with the Holy Spirit and with power; how he went about doing good and healing all who were oppressed by the devil, for God was with him."*

THE ONLY WAY A LOCAL CONGREGATION, WHETHER INDEPENDENT OR DENOMINATIONAL, CAN TRULY BE ALIVE IS TO BE EMPOWERED TO EFFECTIVELY PRESENT THE GOSPEL TO A LOST PERSON.

Even to this day, centuries after Jesus initiated this ministry, we are to continue to be like Him and do what He did. Many (if not most) of the main-line historic churches we know as denominations have closed the door on the Holy Ghost. They have not embraced the baptism of the Holy Spirit or the power which comes with an experience with the Spirit.

Denominations are dying—both spiritually and numerically. The only way a local congregation, whether independent or denominational, can truly be alive is to be empowered to effectively present the Gospel to a lost person.

LIFE AND POWER

Jesus was anointed by the power of the Holy Spirit and He went about doing good, touching lives. The sick were healed, the oppressed were delivered and those possessed by demons were brought out from under the control of Satan. When you personally meet the Holy Spirit, you suddenly have His life and His power.

I am convinced the reason many Methodist, Presbyterian, Baptist, Christian and Reformed churches (among others) are withering is simply because they have shunned the Holy Spirit. When the Spirit is not allowed access you will find a lack of power for miracles.

Many can make a decision to live for Jesus or ask Him to be their Savior, but until the time comes when they have a personal encounter with the Holy Spirit they will lack the power to do the complete work of Jesus.

There are plenty of people who have decided to "sit in" on the Sermon on the Mount, yet only a few who will have the anointing to go forward and change the world.

The accounts recorded in the Book of Acts tell us how the church got its start, and it ought to be the way the church has its finish.

ARE TONGUES REQUIRED?

One of the points of contention between certain Pentecostals and non-charismatic evangelicals regards the issue of speaking with other tongues.

Some believe if you are baptized (or filled) *by* the

Holy Spirit, *of* the Holy Spirit or *in* the Holy Spirit (or the Holy Ghost), you *must* speak in tongues as evidence of the Spirit's work. However, we need to take a close look at how this was described in the early church.

It may come as a surprise to learn that only three times does the Book of Acts—which is our guide—say when you are baptized in or of the Holy Spirit you speak in tongues. At other times it is not mentioned in reference to this gift.

There is ample evidence in the New Testament that the baptism *of* or *in* the Holy Spirit does not necessarily mean you will be using glossolalia—speaking in a strange tongue. This may not sit well with some of my Pentecostal friends, but the Word must be our final authority.

I know many wonderful believers who do not speak in tongues, yet they are every bit as Spirit-filled as those who do. Even more, every Spirit-led person I've met, whether he or she speaks in a heavenly language or not, dissipates what they possess and requires a continually re-filling of the Holy Spirit.

Personally, there are times when I feel empty of the anointing. Those are not good days to be around me! I'm probably going to be grumpy or lacking vision. I may find myself fighting depression and, because of the battle, come dangerously close to losing the war for souls. That's when I need to be filled again. And how is this accomplished? I read, study and ponder the Word. Then I pray and invite the Spirit to come inside.

Because of the emphasis placed on "tongues," some have become fearful of the baptism. They have an aversion (maybe an apprehension) because they may begin speaking in a language known only to God.

BECAUSE OF THE EMPHASIS PLACED ON "TONGUES," SOME HAVE BECOME FEARFUL OF THE BAPTISM.

This is an unnecessary fear. Why should anyone be afraid to communicate in a language which only God comprehends? Isn't it important that God understands? In truth, it is not so crucial whether any other person understands or not (even though there is the gift of interpretation of tongues as recorded in 1 Corinthians 12:10). What's essential is that we communicate with God.

THE KEY VERSE

The key verse of the Book of Acts is found in the first chapter: *"But you will receive power when the Holy Spirit has come upon you; and you will be my witnesses in Jerusalem, in all Judea and, Samaria and to the ends of the earth"* (Acts 1:8).

When Jesus says you will have power to *"be my witnesses"* He is giving a preview of the entire book:

- Chapters 1 through 7 concern power to be witnesses in Jerusalem.
- Chapters 8 through 12 are about power to be witnesses in Judea and Samaria.
- Chapters 13 through 28 focus on power to be witnesses to the ends of the earth.

AN INTERMINGLING OF THE DIVINE AND HUMAN

The "Book of the Acts of the Holy Spirit" is an eye-opening resource. As you read you will discover the embrace of the Spirit.

In addition, if you are studying carefully, you'll become acutely aware of the marvelous intermingling of the divine and the human in action. It is a dynamic the secular world cannot comprehend. Christians can!

Sadly, we have not seen enough of this force in denominational churches—nor in some non-denominational congregations. Instead, what we have often heard and experienced is the flesh expressed by people trying to conjure up the divine.

I've been in some great meetings. *Great* from the standpoint of the size of the audience. *Great* if you consider the music with its beat that seems to propel people to "swing and sway," jump up and down, and become mesmerized by repetition. But, as I looked at the platform, all I saw were performers operating in the flesh.

God despises carnality.

Anyone who stands at a microphone, walks on a platform to sing, touches a keyboard, blows a horn, plays drums, or shakes a tambourine needs to be doing it with the objective of praising God. If they perform for fleshly gratification, the Lord cannot be pleased. Under those conditions, what is supposed to be a move of the Holy Spirit may not be.

WORSHIP WILL OCCUR WHEN AND WHERE THE DIVINE AND THE HUMAN INTERMINGLE AS LED BY THE SPIRIT.

A gathering for worship is not a meeting for entertainment. Worship *will* occur when and where the divine and the human intermingle as led by the Spirit.

NINE DYNAMIC FEATURES OF THE ACTS OF THE APOSTLES

The Book of Acts is a marvelous document which chronicles the promised power of the Spirit after Christ ascended to heaven. There are nine special features of this amazing account:

1. Acts tells us about the church and its source of power and mission.

This important account occupies a prominent place in the Bible because it records the history of the first century church and its extremely close association with

37

both the power and mission of the Holy Spirit.

In truth, you cannot separate God the Father, God the Son, and God the Holy Spirit. Furthermore, you can't separate the Book of Acts from the Trinity—nor the Trinity from the Book of Acts.

Is it any wonder so many denominational churches have lost their zeal and purpose? They treat the vibrant accounts of the outpouring of the Spirit which began in the Upper Room as a relic from the ancient past. It's as if the Acts of the Apostles was for "then," not "now."

Sadly, I have listened to some of my fellow-Methodist ministers give watered-down inspirational talks from the pulpit that would be better suited for the Ladies Wednesday Afternoon Lemonade Society. These are messages containing virtually no Word—and sometimes they don't even mention Jesus. What happened to proclaiming the Gospel?

2. Acts tells us about the baptism of the Holy Spirit and the impartation of power to believers.

The book begins with the post-resurrection ministry of Jesus. During this time He gave a clear directive. The Lord told His followers not to leave Jerusalem, but to wait there for the promise of the Father, *"...for John baptized with water, but you will be baptized with the Holy Spirit not many days from now"* (Acts 1:5). It was then Jesus gave the words of the key verse we have previously mentioned: *"But you will receive power when the Holy Spirit has come upon you; and you will be my witnesses in Jerusalem, in all Judea and Samaria, and to the ends of the earth"* (v.8).

Following the Lord's command, after Jesus ascended to heaven, 120 believers gathered in the Upper Room to await the promise of the Father. As it is recorded, *"And suddenly from heaven there came a sound like the rush of a violent wind, and it filled the entire house where they were sitting. ³Divided tongues, as of fire, appeared among them, and a tongue rested on each of them. All of them were filled with the Holy Spirit and began to speak in other languages, as the Spirit gave them ability"* (Acts 2:2-4).

THIS WAS THE BEGINNING OF A REVIVAL WHICH SWEPT THOUSANDS INTO THE CHURCH —AND IT IS STILL HAPPENING!

This was the beginning of a revival which swept thousands into the church—and it is still happening!

3. Acts contains inspired early church messages and sermons.

Beginning with the message Peter delivered to an amazed audience following the outpouring of the Spirit, you will never find a clearer presentation of the Gospel than the sermons recorded in Acts. Three thousand were added to the church that day.

This is why I urge ministers and evangelists to immerse themselves in the messages of Acts.

In chapter 7, Stephen, *"filled with the Holy Spirit"* (Acts 7:55) presented the Sanhedrin with an overview of the work of God from Abraham to Christ.

Today, we have many so-called "evangelists" who have wide appeal. However, marketing skills do not guarantee the Gospel has been faithfully proclaimed. We need a return to the power of the Spirit as found in these early messages.

4. Acts is a handbook on prayer.

The church seems to have forgotten how to pray. In

THE CHURCH SEEMS TO HAVE FORGOTTEN HOW TO PRAY.

fact, many congregations *never* have prayer meetings—and if they do it is an anemic exercise. A few will gather in a circle and whoever can think of a "sentence prayer" will utter a few words.

Where are the churches with people who come to an altar and stay until there is a genuine breakthrough—until the devil and his demons are moved from blocking the space between you and the throne of God?

When I was just a young preacher, I heard an

elderly minister say, "Praying is like pulling on a rope. You just keep tugging and tugging until you feel somebody pulling back on the other end. That's prayer!"

In the Book of the Acts, prayer was a serious matter:

- In the midst of miracles, when the believers *"had prayed, the place in which they were gathered together was shaken; and they were all filled with the Holy Spirit and spoke the word of God with boldness"* (Acts 4:31).
- When Peter was in prison, *"The church prayed fervently to God for him"* (Acts 12:5). What was the result? His chains fell off and he was free man!
- Again, when Paul and Silas were thrown in jail, about midnight they were *"praying and singing hymns to God"* (Acts 16:25). Suddenly there was such a violent earthquake, the prison doors flew open wide.

I believe a return to fervent, regular prayer will fill empty churches and usher in a return of the Spirit's anointing.

5. Acts records signs, wonders and miracles.
Jesus was no longer physically present, yet what He

said concerning the "signs" which would follow those who believed was certainly evident in the Acts of the Apostles. At every turn, sick bodies were being healed and evil spirits were cast out.

Here's what is significant: the signs, wonders and miracles accompanied the proclamation of the Gospel. When the crippled beggar was healed in the presence of Peter and John (Acts 3), Peter turned to the crowd and proclaimed, *"Repent therefore, and turn to God so that your sins may be wiped out, so that times of refreshing may come from the presence of the Lord, and that he may send the Messiah appointed for you, that is, Jesus"* (Acts 3:19-20).

The story continues in chapter 4 where we find Peter and John in trouble because they were proclaiming that in Jesus there is resurrection from the dead. The priests, the captain of the temple, and Sadducees were extremely annoyed and held them in custody until the next day. Yet, something powerful was happening. Scripture records, *"Many of those who heard the word believed and they numbered about 5,000 and praised God"* (Acts 4:4).

The miracles and the message were both present.

Could the lack of miracles in churches today be because the Gospel is being preached with the intellect instead of the Spirit? I believe the soul (mental) area of man must move out of the way and allow the spirit side to gush forth with the right message. We need to proclaim Jesus with *power*—His shed blood, the stripes, the cross, the empty tomb, His ascension to the Father and His soon return.

This is an invitation for signs and wonders.

6. Acts shows us how to respond to persecution.

In the midst of miracles we find the followers of Christ accused, threatened, beaten and imprisoned as the result of both religious and secular opposition.

This should not come as a surprise since Jesus said, *"Blessed are you when people revile you and utter all kinds of evil against you falsely on my account"* (Matthew 5:11).

Don't be dismayed. In the next verse, Jesus explains: *"Rejoice and be glad, for your reward is great in heaven, for in the same way they persecuted the prophets who were before you"* (v.12).

IF WE PLAN TO MAKE A MARK FOR THE KINGDOM, WE NEED TO EXPECT THE DARTS AND ARROWS.

Of course, we need to pray that God gives us favor with men in all we say and do, but if we plan to make a mark for the kingdom, we need to expect the darts and arrows.

Regardless of the circumstances, I believe God's favor can work for us just as it did for Moses and the

Israelites. The plunder they took from the Egyptians became part of the tabernacle built for the glory of God.

When persecution comes, get ready for blessing!

7. Acts demonstrates how we are to love "God's chosen people."

In the sight of the Lord, the Jews are given high priority. The first message Peter delivered after coming out of the Upper Room, began with these words: *"Men of Judea and all who live in Jerusalem, let this be known to you, and listen to what I say"* (Acts 2:14).

Peter then reminded them of the words of the prophet Joel, that in the last days God would pour out His Spirit on all people (v.17).

Paul, after his dramatic conversion, began sharing Christ—starting with the Jews and continuing to *all* people. He *"declared first to those in Damascus, then in Jerusalem and throughout the countryside of Judea, and also to the Gentiles, that they should repent and turn to God and do deeds consistent with repentance"* (Acts 26:20).

This same principle is later related by the Apostle Paul to the Romans: *"For I am not ashamed of the Gospel; it is the power of God for salvation to everyone who has faith: to the Jew first and also to the Greek"* (Romans 1:16).

Today, with the Middle East embroiled in

bloodshed, we are to pray for the peace of Jerusalem.

8. Acts details the role of women in the church.

Many are surprised to find the prominent place given to women as ministry was established in the first century. When the 120 believers gathered to wait for the promised Holy Spirit, it wasn't a "men only" assembly. The Bible tells us they were *"devoting themselves to prayer, together with certain women, including Mary the mother of Jesus"* (Acts 1:14).

MANY ARE SURPRISED TO FIND THE PROMINENT PLACE GIVEN TO WOMEN AS MINISTRY WAS ESTABLISHED IN THE FIRST CENTURY.

Mary—the mother of John Mark—was involved in a ministry of hospitality to the emerging Christian church (Acts 12:12).

Paul's first convert at Philippi was a businesswoman named Lydia—who opened her home to the apostle. Scripture records that *"she and her household were baptized"* (Acts 16:15). She became an important voice to the new believers in that city.

In Athens, Damaris became a follower of Christ (Acts 17:34).

The four daughters of Phillip the evangelist were used in prophetic ministry (Acts 21:9).

What is chronicled in Acts is just the beginning of the place of women in the on-going work of the church. Thank God, it continues to this day.

9. Acts records the story of triumph and victory.

In this glorious account there was no barrier which could halt the advance of the Gospel—not political opposition, religious ritual, cultural bias or racial prejudice.

At every turn roadblocks were placed in the way of the followers of Christ, yet the message marched forward. Even the death of Stephen couldn't stop these believers. With great conviction and passion they took the message to city after city.

Then, after the miraculous conversion of Saul on the road to Damacus (Acts 9), he became the Apostle Paul—the great evangelist whose dramatic missionary journeys begin in Acts and continue through the New Testament.

The triumphs far outweighed the trials. The book ends with Paul under arrest in Rome, yet still preaching. In fact, in the last verse of Acts we find the apostle *"proclaiming the kingdom of God and teaching about the Lord Jesus Christ with all boldness"* (Acts 28:31).

That's victory!

THE STORY CONTINUES

Acts tells us what the church must be and do—in

any generation. Even though the accounts are limited to 28 chapters, the book is still being written and we are part of it!

Those who say, "The baptism of the Holy Spirit was only for the first century church," and "miracles no longer happen," offer a meaningless argument. They need to talk to a person who has had the experience.

When Jesus said His followers would receive power from on high, He meant every word. The same messages from our Master are sent to us through the communication of the Holy Spirit—who still comes upon people just as on the Day of Pentecost.

As we will see, the power promised by Jesus is very much alive—and continues to touch millions around the world.

MY PRAYER FOR YOU

Holy Spirit, I thank you for Your presence. I know You are watching over the reader of these pages. Reach down and touch this life as only You can. May the Word come alive through Your Spirit today.

CHAPTER 3

THE POWER OF ASSOCIATION

As a youngster, when I got into trouble by choosing the wrong friends, my mother would call me aside and caution, "Remember Bud (my childhood nickname), birds of a feather, flock together." And if she saw real problems looming on the horizon, I was warned: "If you lay down with dogs, you'll get up with fleas."

I knew what she meant; it had to do with the power of association. As I grew older, I cherished her advice and began to understand the value of linking my life with the right individuals.

Today, in business, education, family life and our interaction with fellow-believers, we see the strength which results from healthy relationships.

A DIVINE UNION

Fellowship is not a new phenomenon. In fact, before the universe was ever spun into space, there was a divine union alive and very much at work. Let me explain.

Most Christians associate the Holy Spirit with the New Testament—and the outpouring of power that followed the Upper Room experience. A closer look at the Word, however, reveals the Third Person of the Trinity was present from the foundation of the world.

The second verse of Genesis gives this description of creation: *"And the earth was without form, and void; and darkness was upon the face of the deep. And the Spirit of God moved upon the face of the waters"* (Genesis 1:2 KJV).

SPECIFICALLY, THE HOLY SPIRIT IS MENTIONED IN 22 OF THE OLD TESTAMENT BOOKS.

Specifically, the Holy Spirit is mentioned in 22 of the Old Testament books.

What we are talking about is not "something" that was invented. The Holy Spirit is a *person*, not an object nor a *thing*. He is very much alive and has been part of the Godhead from *before* the beginning. Just as God has always been, so has the Holy Spirit. They are "one" (Malachi 2:15).

When the Creator declared, *"Let there be light"*

(Genesis 1:3), the Spirit was present. Prior to this moment, time was not relevant and nothing was needed to separate night from day, darkness from light.

It is impossible for our finite minds to grasp the infinite—to stretch our intellect and think about "always." Why? Because we focus on a moment in time, the blink of an eye.

We can hardly imagine God being so all-encompassing that before there was anything, He filled *everything*. Our thought process can't fathom a God so unlimited He can give and give for eons and never be diminished.

A CONFERENCE IN THE HEAVENLIES

When you consider the omniscient, omnipotent, omnipresent Father, always remember the Holy Spirit and God the Son have forever existed together in perfect fellowship—and always will. It is their association which makes possible our eternal life.

At a moment before this earth was formed, the three members of the Godhead made a divine decision that the Son would be born into the world as a man. He would be Jesus of Nazareth, with God incarnate in Him. Even more, Jesus would pay the entire penalty for the sins of the whole world.

Can you envision what it must have been like when this meeting took place? It happened at a moment we can't identify because it was always the plan of the

Father, the Son and the Holy Spirit for Christ to come into the physical world and become the ultimate sacrifice for our redemption.

Out of this pure union—a flawless association—came an act which looked to be imperfect because of the way Jesus had to suffer and die. Yet, God knew the solution necessary for sin.

Today, it is the Holy Spirit who draws men to the Son and who leads, comforts and empowers believers. This same Spirit has been present at every major turning point in the world's history.

THE HOLY SPIRIT AND THE CREATION OF BEAUTY

Try as we might, it is impossible for man to recreate a picturesque sunset or a dramatic mountain range. These are formed by a power far greater than human imagination.

Some may think beauty is conjured up in the make-up salons of Hollywood or in the studio of a famous artist. At best, these talented individuals can only attempt to enhance what has been created by a higher power.

The Bible makes it clear the Holy Spirit is involved with the Godhead in an awesome display of beauty. *"By his Spirit he has garnished the heavens"* (Job 26:13 KJV). And we know, *"The heavens declare the glory of God; and the firmament showeth his handiwork"* (Psalm19:1 KJV).

THE HOLY SPIRIT AND THE ANIMAL WORLD

The next time you see a flock of geese flying overhead or spot a deer darting through a forest, pause and consider that all creatures—large and small—were co-created by the Spirit.

The psalmist writes: *"O Lord, how manifold are your works! In wisdom you have made them all; the earth is full of your creatures. Yonder is the sea, great and wide, creeping things innumerable are there, living things both small and great...When you send forth your spirit, they are created; and you renew the face of the ground"* (Psalm 104:24,30).

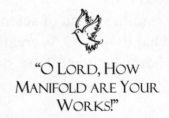

"O LORD, HOW MANIFOLD ARE YOUR WORKS!"

How are they made? By God sending forth His Spirit!

THE HOLY SPIRIT AND THE CREATION OF SUBSTANCE

All physical matter, even an object so minute it can't be seen with the naked eye, has been created in association with God's Holy Spirit.

To better understand the role of the Spirit on the physical earth, consider the words spoken through the prophet Isaiah: *"For the palace will be forsaken, the populous city deserted; the hill and the watchtower will become dens forever...until a spirit from on high is poured out on us, and the wilderness becomes a fruitful field, and the fruitful field is deemed a forest. Then justice will dwell in the wilderness, and righteousness abide in the fruitful field"* (Isaiah 32:14-16).

In the arena of science there are those working on what they think is creation, yet it is not. For example, pharmaceutical labs do not create *anything*, they merely re-arrange elements a higher power has made available.

SADLY, MANY MISUSE WHAT GOD INTENDS FOR GOOD.

Sadly, many misuse what God intends for good. Let me elaborate. A chemist can concoct a so-called performance enhancing drug that, without being detected, can produce Olympic Gold Medal champions and baseball home run heroes. Yet, the long-term consequences of "playing god" with drugs can lead to untold physical harm—even death.

There's great danger in altering what God has made.

THE HOLY SPIRIT AND
THE CREATION OF REST

It is a scientific fact that the DNA in a living man or woman breaks down over time. Some estimate it is designed to last about 120 years.

This is the amount of time God declared in Genesis before He would withdraw His Spirit from mankind. The Lord said, *"My spirit shall not always strive with man, for that he also is flesh: yet his days shall be an hundred and twenty years"*(Genesis 6:3 KJV).

The reason many "shut down" before this stated age is because they don't know how to participate in God's divine rest—which was created by His Spirit. This is evident in the words of Isaiah. Speaking of Moses and the children of Israel, he asks, *"Where is the one who brought them up out of the sea with the shepherds of his flock? Where is the one who put within them his holy spirit...who led them through the depths? Like a horse in the desert, they did not stumble. Like cattle that go down into the valley, the spirit of the Lord gave them rest"* (Isaiah 63:11, 13-14).

I feel for people who say, "I just can't sleep." One friend I know averages only four hours a night.

If you have the ability to rest peacefully, be thankful. You are participating in something the Godhead has made and to which we are entitled. This rejuvenation process is a precious gift of the Spirit we need to continually seek.

THE HOLY SPIRIT AND THE CREATION OF MAN

You are more than the result of a "twinkle in your father's eye." Without God's Spirit you would not have been conceived. As Job writes, *"The spirit of God hath made me, and the breath of the Almighty hath given me life"* (Job 33:4 KJV).

This was also true in the coming to earth of the Son of God. Scripture records, *"Now the birth of Jesus the Messiah took place in this way. When his mother Mary had been engaged to Joseph, but before they lived together, she was found to be with child from the Holy Spirit"* (Matthew 1:18).

In our ministry, I have witnessed God's creative Spirit at work.

A lovely couple from Georgia with a music ministry visited a church I pastored in Missouri. They had one son and desperately wanted another child, but the doctor had essentially told them, "You can't. You won't. It's not going to happen." He counseled, "If you want another child, you should seriously consider adoption."

I didn't know these facts when they sang in our church one Sunday. Then, as I began my message, I stopped, walked down in front of the congregation and announced, "The Holy Spirit has just led me to change my message."

I asked the people to turn with me to the book of James and I began sharing scriptures regarding anointing with oil.

There was a small vase of oil on the communion table, and although our guests had ministered in many churches, they had never before seen anointing oil.

The woman was seated next to my wife in the second row. At the close of the service, she asked my wife to accompany her to the front for prayer. As she approached, I covered the

"LYDIA, WHAT CAN I PRAY WITH YOU ABOUT?"

microphone and asked, "Lydia, what can I pray with you about?"

Quietly, she answered, "I want to get pregnant."

Immediately, I anointed her with oil, placed my hands on her head and began to call upon God. After a few moments, I backed up and commented, "I once saw a Spirit-filled Baptist minister do this and feel impressed to follow his example."

With that said, I pointed right at her stomach and declared, "I rebuke the spirit of barrenness from your womb in the Name of Jesus."

It was about ten months later she gave birth to a

healthy son.

Since God's Spirit is the creator of man, it wasn't my words which began a miracle—but perhaps it was my obedience.

THE HOLY SPIRIT AND THE CREATION OF DEATH

Acts 5 reveals the tragic story of Ananias and Sapphira who lied about how much money should have been brought to the Christian community.

Peter asked Ananias, *"Why has Satan filled your heart to lie to the Holy Spirit and to keep back part of the proceeds of the land? While it remained unsold, did it not remain your own? And after it was sold, were not the proceeds at your disposal? How is it that you have contrived this deed in your heart? You did not lie to us but to God!"* (Acts 5:3-4).

When Ananias heard this, he fell down and died (v.5).

About three hours later his wife arrived on the scene, not knowing what had taken place. Peter said to her, "Tell me whether you and your husband sold the land for such and such a price." And she responded, "Yes, that was the amount."

Then Peter asked Sapphira, *"How is it that you have agreed together to put the Spirit of the Lord to the test? Look, the feet of those who have buried your husband are at the door, and they will carry you out"* (v.9).

At that moment she also died—because of lying to the Holy Spirit.

If God had not created death, there would be none (in spite of those who attribute death to Satan). Remember, He said, *"My spirit shall not always strive with man"* (Genesis 6:3 KJV).

Thank God, there will come a day when this scourge is eradicated. Scripture declares He will *"wipe every tear from their eyes. Death will be no more; mourning and crying and pain will be no more"* (Revelation 21:4).

Why? Because this was agreed upon by the Father, Son, and Holy Spirit long before this earth came into existence.

THE HOLY SPIRIT AND EVANGELISM

The great outpouring of the Spirit in the early days of the twentieth century was not meant for America alone. The Holy Spirit is at the heart of the Great Commission—to reach the nations of the world with the Gospel.

> THE HOLY SPIRIT IS AT THE HEART OF THE GREAT COMMISSION—TO REACH THE NATIONS OF THE WORLD WITH THE GOSPEL.

I praise God when I hear how the Body of Christ is growing rapidly in Africa, Asia and South America.

Even more, I pray this same Spirit will return to our shores with a greater power than anything we have previously experienced. May it revitalize the church and profoundly affect every aspect of our government and society.

The only effective way to preach the Gospel is to personally know the Spirit of Truth. Never forget the words of Jesus: *"When the Advocate comes, whom I will send to you from the Father, the Spirit of truth who comes from the Father, he will testify on my behalf"* (John 15:26).

It is not you who is evangelizing, it is the Spirit speaking *through* you.

AN ETERNAL ASSOCIATION

As you follow the career of the Holy Spirit, you discover He was not only involved in the creation of the Second Adam and the birth of the church, He was also present at the creation of the Word.

Since all scripture is inspired by God, the Spirit breathed life into the words which found their way into our Holy Bible.

While He has been present with the Godhead in all of these creative acts, He has also been greatly involved with man.

In the Old Testament, the Spirit would rest upon the tabernacle and visit the saints of God, then move on.

In the New Testament, after Christ's ascension to heaven, there was a great change. As promised by Jesus, the Holy Spirit literally *dwelt* in the lives of the disciples and early Christians—and is still alive in the hearts of believers today.

Now, the Spirit rests upon the church—of which we are a part. Yet it takes more than becoming a member of a local congregation to experience His presence. It is personal, and begins with salvation. The Lord *"saved us, not because of any works of righteousness that we had done, but according to his mercy, through the water of rebirth and renewal by the Holy Spirit"* (Titus 3:5).

What is next on the horizon? This same Spirit which was present at the foundation of the world will also be involved in the creation of *"new heavens and a new earth"* (2 Pet 3:13 KJV). In these last days, we must *"listen to what the Spirit is saying to the churches"* (Revelation 2:7).

I invite you to welcome the Holy Spirit into your life. If you will reach for His embrace, you will be a participant in this divine association.

MY PRAYER FOR YOU
*I pray the same Spirit which
is present in all of God's creation will
bless you with His presence—beyond
anything you can ask or think.*

CHAPTER 4

YOU HAVE AN ADVOCATE

Rather than using force, the Holy Spirit *compels* you to move toward the vision the Father has placed in your heart. He gives you the passion and drive to succeed at your God-given task—no matter how difficult it may seem. The details may not be crystal clear, yet the Spirit gives a peace about the direction you are headed.

Jesus taught His followers the importance of fully understanding that the Almighty is "Spirit."

Prior to Jesus' arrest, trial and crucifixion, He comforted the disciples by telling them not to allow their hearts to be troubled: *"Believe in God, believe also in me. In my Father's house there are many dwelling places. If it were not so, would I have told you that I go to prepare a place for you? And if I go and*

63

prepare a place for you, I will come again and will take you to myself, so that where I am, there you may be also" (John 14-1-3).

In this significant passage, Jesus was explaining it is only by faith in God, who is unseen (Spirit), that His followers could have any confidence in what He is telling them about a place they could not see.

On this same occasion, Philip said to Him, *"Lord, show us the Father and we will be satisfied"* (v.8).

Jesus gave a rather long answer, yet it is extremely important since it addresses the issue of the Spirit indwelling man—how an invisible God could live in a physical being.

The Lord answered Philip, *"Have I been with you all this time, Philip, and you still do not know me? Whoever has seen me has seen the Father. How can you say, 'Show us the Father'? Do you not believe that I am in the Father and the Father is in me? The words that I say to you I do not speak on my own; but the Father who dwells in me does his works. Believe me that I am in the Father and the Father is in me; but if you do not, then believe me because of the works themselves. Very truly, I tell you, the one who believes in me will also do the works that I do and, in fact, will do greater works than these, because I am going to the Father. I will do whatever you ask in my name, so that the Father may be glorified in the Son. If in my name you ask me for anything, I will do it"* (John 14:9-14).

"I Will Ask the Father"

Just because we cannot see God, doesn't mean He is non-existent. The same is true of heaven. We do not have to walk on its streets of gold in order to believe it is a physical place. No. We have faith in the Word and know what Jesus says is true.

It was immediately after this question-answer session with the disciples Jesus promised to send the Holy Spirit to dwell among us

Just Because We Cannot See God, Doesn't Mean He is Non-Existent.

after His death, resurrection and ascension (John 14:15-31).

The disciples knew Jesus was "real" because they walked and talked with Him. Then, they passed their-first-hand accounts and eye-witness reports on to those who wrote the Gospels and Acts.

Today, the way we are able to understand the reality of God, Jesus and eternity is through the person of the Holy Spirit. Only He can teach us the truth of invisible, spiritual matters.

Jesus gave this directive—accompanied by a powerful promise: *"If you love me, you will keep my commandments. And I will ask the Father, and he will give you another Advocate, to be with you forever. This is the Spirit of truth, whom the world cannot receive, because it neither sees him nor knows him. You know him, because he abides with you, and he will be in you"* (John 14:15-17).

I cannot overemphasize the importance of these words. If you love Jesus, based on what the Word of God says, you will keep the "commandments" of Jesus. We are not referring to the Ten Commandments given to Moses, rather the enlargement of them which includes everything Jesus commanded.

This is the key to receiving the Spirit of Truth.

YOUR SOURCE OF TRUTH

I smile when I think of some people who attempt to personally teach "Spiritual gifts." Friend, these things cannot be taught by man—only by the Spirit Himself.

As Jesus told the disciples, *"I have said these things to you while I am still with you. But the Advocate, the Holy Spirit, whom the Father will send in my name, will teach you everything, and remind you of all that I have said to you"* (John 15:25-26).

If the Holy Spirit does not teach us what Jesus is like, what He has accomplished, where He is and what His future plans entail, how can we ever know the Father or have any peace concerning what happens after death?

When you allow yourself to be touched by the Spirit, you have an Instructor who will always tell you the absolute, unvarnished truth.

DOING THE FATHER'S WORK

During the ministry of Jesus on earth, religious leaders constantly questioned Him concerning Old Testament law—attempting to corner Him. His answers confounded them because He didn't preach legalism, but love.

When He was asked, "What is the greatest commandment in the law?" Jesus responded by stating, *"'You shall love the Lord your God with all your heart, and with all your soul, and with all your mind.' This is*

"WHAT IS THE GREATEST COMMANDMENT IN THE LAW?"

the greatest and first commandment. And a second is like it: 'You shall love your neighbor as yourself'" (Matthew 22:37-39).

On this and other occasions, Jesus emphasized doing the work of the Father on earth—to visit the sick, remember those in prison, to provide food, water and clothing to people in need. In other words, we are to *do* the commandments and support those who have been called to a ministry of helps.

In my denomination it is expected for every member of the church to be a minister, but only some are set apart and ordained to be in full time service as "professionals" (for lack of a better word).

If we fail to follow His command and become involved, why would He be under any obligation to give us another Advocate—the Holy Spirit?

The word Advocate refers to someone who will stand with us, regardless of the nature of our problem.

"HE WILL BE IN YOU"

I recently had a couple come to my office asking for my help. They were negotiating to purchase a piece of property which included a store building they wanted to transform into a center for Christian services, Bible study and family counseling.

THE SPIRIT IS NETHER INTERESTED IN NOR OBLIGATED TO DO ANYTHING WHICH DOES NOT HONOR JESUS.

Their financial offer had been accepted, but they faced hurdles with the city over regulations. The number one issue was presenting proof they represented an organized ministry and were an approved non-profit organization. As president of Acts Ministry, they came to me so I could become their advocate to the local officials—which I was more than happy to do.

This is exactly what the Holy Spirit does for you and me; He stands with us. However, we need to be aware the Spirit is neither interested in nor obligated to do anything which does not honor Jesus.

Never forget what the Lord told His disciples as He was carrying on a conversation with Phillip. He said: *"You know him* [the Holy Spirit] *because he abides with you, and he will be in you"* (John 14:17).

Certainly, the Spirit can be present in people who may not be fully engaged in ministry or matured in their walk with the Lord. He is living in the same house, and abiding in the same natural surroundings. However, when He is *in* you, He will be operating *through* you.

ALIVE AND EFFECTIVE!

Scripture makes it clear that the Son of God is the one who anoints and the Holy Spirit *carries* the anointing, making it alive and effective. John the disciple writes: *"As for you, the anointing that you receive from him abides in you, and so you do not need anyone to teach you. But as his anointing teaches you about all things, and is true and is not a lie, and just as it has taught you, abide in him"* 1 John 2:27).

If you have the presence of the living Christ in you, there is an anointing that will teach you. This does not mean you should shun instruction or avoid sitting under the teaching of a minister of the Gospel. Otherwise Paul would not have written that in the church there would be apostles, prophets, evangelists, pastors and teachers (Ephesians 4:11).

We are to cooperate and share with those who are placed in the body as teachers. However, there will be times you need a special word from heaven only the Spirit can provide.

WHO IS CALLING?

I believe disunity in the body of Christ is due, in part, to the fact some people hear a Spirit-filled, Spirit-led teacher, but do not listen with the aid of the Holy Spirit. Rather than accepting spoken truth, they rely on their own preconceived ideas.

There are hundreds of religious denominations— each with a unique position on various doctrines of the Bible. Can they all be right? Hardly! This is why we need to ask the Holy Spirit to lead us "into all truth."

The Spirit will not "team-teach" with those who are self-appointed to a place of authority in the church. There are far too many who like the idea of spiritual leadership and have called themselves into ministry.

After observing some who have tried and failed, I have concluded that a person who loves the idea of being involved in spiritual leadership and desires desperately to be a minister is probably calling him or herself. On the other hand, those God calls usually hold back for a lengthy period of time until they feel compelled to take a bold step—something not of their own choosing.

NOT MY CHOICE

As I mentioned earlier, I was called to preach when I was only nine years old, yet, as I entered college, I was determined to go into medicine.

At the age of 19, I was converted to Christ and it was only then I answered the call to ministry. In my case, I was *called* before being *converted!* The Holy Spirit compelled me to do something I was running from. So midway in my college experience, I left my pre-med studies and began academic pursuits that would lead me toward the ministry.

You are Under no Obligation to Listen to a Teacher who is Self-Appointed.

If it had been *my* choice, I would now likely be a retired surgeon playing golf at a country club. However, the Lord had other plans.

You are under no obligation to listen to a teacher who is self-appointed, and you will know the difference when the anointing of God's Spirit is active and alive within you.

A PANORAMIC VIEW

Much of the information which has been coming to the body of Christ has arrived through what I would call a "constriction." The truth has been narrowed and tightened until we are only receiving a small "blink" of light—not the complete picture.

I am no photographer, so I was surprised to learn that you could flip a switch on a camera and take a panoramic view. This is what the Lord desires for His people—a complete vista of what the Spirit is wanting to accomplish; not the narrow image of a dogmatic teacher who focuses on one or two scriptures to support his mistaken beliefs.

The big picture given by your Advocate, Teacher and Guide, provides enough information so you won't have to carry a set of rules in your vest pocket or purse.

The second chapter of 1st John begins with what I call "cage rattling" verses. *"My little children, I am writing these things to you so that you may not sin. But if anyone does sin, we have an advocate with the Father, Jesus Christ the righteous; and he is the atoning sacrifice for our sins, and not for ours only but also for the sins of the whole world"* (1 John 2:1-2}.

ANOTHER HELPER

Jesus is a lawyer and a defense attorney representing us before Almighty God. In other words, Jesus came as not only the sacrifice for sin, but as an Advocate for our transgressions. And He did this for everyone. *"God so loved the world of persons that He gave his only begotten Son, so that if we believe in Him we would not need to perish but we could have eternal life"* (Paraphrase of John 3:16).

It is vital we understand the significance of what Jesus said before He returned to His Father in heaven. He promised to send *another* helper—the Holy Spirit—who would continue His work on earth as our Advocate, Paraclete and Defender.

Jesus ascended to sit at the right hand of the Father, but we were not left comfortless. There is someone who continues to plead our cause and represent us—the Third Person of the Trinity, the Holy Spirit.

I get excited every time I think of God's marvelous plan!

MY PRAYER FOR YOU
*I am agreeing with you today that the Holy
Spirit will be present as your Helper and Advocate.
Regardless of the trials you face, I pray you will feel
His presence and rest in the assurance all
things are working together for your good.*

CHAPTER 5

YOUR DIRECT CONNECTION TO THE FATHER

F reedom of worship is one of the founding principles of our nation—an important part of the fabric which holds America together. This religious tolerance allows each of us to express our faith in a wide variety of ways. As a result, there are those who kneel quietly, while others raise their hands and voices in exuberant, demonstrative praise.

The common objective which unites all believers is the focus on the Almighty, All-Powerful, Creator of the Universe. Through prayer, praise and worship, we gather together to honor the Lord.

However, for practically all of recorded history, questions involving style of worship have constantly swirled around believers.

"In Spirit and Truth"

I'm sure you recall the story of Jesus traveling from Jerusalem to Galilee and stopping in Samaria to have a drink at Jacob's well. While there, He struck up a conversation with a Samaritan woman. The very fact He spoke to her was controversial since the people of Samaria were considered by many Jews to be a mongrel race.

JESUS OFFERED THE WOMAN "LIVING WATER" SO SHE WOULD NEVER THIRST AGAIN.

We remember the story because Jesus offered the woman "living water" so she would never thirst again. Yet, as the conversation continues, they began talking about worship.

The woman said to Him, *"Sir, I see that you are a prophet. Our ancestors worshiped on this mountain, but you say that the place where people must worship is in Jerusalem"* (John 4:19-20).

Jesus clarified the query with this response: *"Woman, believe me, the hour is coming when you will worship the Father neither on this mountain nor in Jerusalem. You worship what you do not know; we worship what we know, for salvation is from the Jews. But the hour is coming, and is now here, when the true worshipers will worship the Father in spirit and truth, for the Father seeks such as these to worship him"* (vv.21-23). And He added, *"God is spirit, and those who worship him must worship in spirit and truth"* (v.24).

"GOD IS A SPIRIT, AND THOSE WHO WORSHIP HIM MUST WORSHIP HIM IN SPIRIT AND TRUTH."

This was an astounding statement—especially to a woman whose people bowed before multiple deities and had a legacy dating back to the times of King Solomon.

BRIDGING THE GAP

Solomon has etched a place in both secular and biblical history as the wealthiest man who ever lived—also one of the wisest. Yet, in spite of his wisdom, he made mistakes because of his weakness for women. Many argue there were political reasons behind his choice of wives, especially considering he married several women who were not of Jewish heritage.

One fact is clear. Solomon gave his wives the freedom to worship as they pleased and even built places of worship dedicated to "other gods."

There were *"high places,"* as referred to in the Old Testament (1 Kings 3:3; 2 Kings 23:13), where they employed a variety of worship practices that were totally incompatible with the God of the Hebrews. All sorts of evil customs were allowed—especially in the northern part of the kingdom.

From his union with these women of different beliefs, the Samaritan people had their origin. As you can imagine, Jews would have little to do with the people of Samaria because they were considered part of a heathen (often pagan) style of worship.

In the New Testament, centuries later, we find Jesus bridging the gap and telling a Samarian of the vital role the Spirit plays in worship—reaching out toward God.

HERE COMES THE CLOUD!

As both an observer and a participant in the church of our day, I can tell you with authority the body of Christ is sorely lacking in unity. The wholeness I am speaking of can only be understood through worship.

Just as the oboe is used to tune all other instruments in a symphony, the people of God need to align themselves through worship. We must be heard in unison through praise and thanksgiving to the Lord.

In Solomon's time, when the great temple was built, the house of the Lord was filled with what the Bible describes as "a cloud." After the elders brought the ark of the covenant to the new temple, the priests placed it in the inner sanctuary. Then, when they came out of the holy place, scripture records: *"...a cloud filled the house of the Lord, so that the priests could not stand to minister because of the cloud; for the glory of the Lord filled the house"* (1 Kings 8:10-11).

This is significant because during the wilderness wanderings, the children of Israel walked by sight. By day they could see the cloud and by night they followed the pillar of fire. When the cloud or fire moved, so did they.

Finally, when they arrived at the Jordan River and crossed over, they built a monument of stones and called it Gilgal. This was a major turning point in the history of God's people. The fire lifted and the cloud dissipated. From this time forward they were

FROM THIS TIME FORWARD, THEY WERE EXPECTED —AS WE ARE— TO WALK BY FAITH INSTEAD OF BY SIGHT.

expected—as are we—to walk by faith instead of by sight (2 Corinthians.5:7).

"SLAIN IN THE SPIRIT"

Many years later, God allowed Solomon to construct the magnificent temple even though it was built by a man with numerous ungodly characteristics—his choice of wives being one of them.

What made the temple beautiful was much more than the ornate craftsmanship or the wealth of the man who built it. This sanctuary was marvelous because of what took place inside—the praise and worship of the people.

There was *unity of spirit* in these faith-filled individuals and the house of the Lord was permeated with a holy cloud. It does not surprise me the presence of God was so strong the priests *"could not stand to minister."* Today, we call this being "slain in the Spirit."

WHAT A MOMENT IT MUST HAVE BEEN AS THE MUSIC, THE PRAISE, THE WORSHIP AND THE CLOUD WERE JOINED TOGETHER!

What a moment it must have been as the music, the praise, the worship and the cloud were joined together! The presence of the Lord God of Israel had returned in person and the priests who were sanctified—set apart for a holy use—could not stand on their own two feet. They fell before the Lord.

ENCOUNTERING GOD

Even *before* Solomon, altars were built by those who often had "unclean hands." His father, David, was a man of bloodshed who made enough human mistakes to fill several chapters of the Bible, yet the Lord continued to use him in marvelous ways.

You see, God has always embraced His people

through the Holy Spirit—even though it took forms which were somewhat different than those experienced by you and me.

Before Solomon's Temple, the Tabernacle was built by the children of Israel in the wilderness and had elements which relate to the church today.

BEFORE SOLOMON'S TEMPLE, THE TABERNACLE WAS BUILT BY THE CHILDREN OF ISRAEL IN THE WILDERNESS AND HAD ELEMENTS WHICH RELATE TO THE CHURCH TODAY.

The Tabernacle had an Outer Court. It was here the priest would cleanse himself physically—the flesh. The Inner Court was called the Way of Holiness and the place to begin focusing on God. The priest would no longer think about common things, but instead would turn his attention to the world above so his soul would become quiet.

Finally, he would enter into the Holy of Holies. This was the "inner place" where he would engage in spiritual matters and God could be encountered.

PREPARE FOR THE SANCTUARY

The church of Century 21 has similar vestiges. The foyer of the current church building is in essence the outer court of the tabernacle. It is in this entryway you are to place your flesh under subjection.

What many people call the sanctuary is actually the *nave*. Seated in the pews of the church is where we should prepare our mind and soul to hear about God—not dwelling or worrying over last week's problems or the pot roast simmering on the stove. In one church I noticed a small sign: "Enter to worship and depart to serve. During the prelude, please be quiet and remain in an attitude of prayer." It is not a place for idle conversation with friends or other mundane activities.

WITHOUT YOUR SOUL BEING PREPARED, YOU SHOULD NOT APPROACH THE SANCTUARY.

Without your soul being prepared, you should not approach the *sanctuary*—the front of the church or around the communion table (some call it the altar). This is where we meet God.

Too many people have a habit of running to the altar without thought or preparation. It is a serious matter to come into this area with carnal attitudes and actions.

I believe there is a relationship between priests, rabbis, the five-fold ministries (Ephesians 4:11) and our worship experience.

God calls some and sets them in the church to be apostles, prophets, evangelists, pastors and teachers. Personally, I was called to preach the Gospel. In the process, I have filled several roles in ministry. For example:

- I was never truly called to be a pastor, yet I have been the shepherd of many flocks.
- Nor was I specifically called to be an evangelist, but I have preached revivals in numerous parts of the nation.
- I wasn't called to be an apostle, yet I am currently involved in an apostolic ministry.

When we are totally yielded to the Holy Spirit, He will lead us into areas to better prepare us for our mission—to present ourselves in service as an act of worship to the Lord.

"JOINED TOGETHER"

Throughout the Old Testament we read detailed descriptions of how the people made sacrifices to the Lord and brought offerings. Today, we present the Lord's tithe and our gifts to Him—not out of duty, rather as an act of praise and worship. As every element of ministry flows together in unity, the "cloud," God's anointing and presence fills the house. As Paul writes: *"In him the whole structure is joined together and grows into a holy temple in the Lord; in whom you also are built together spiritually into a dwelling place for God"* (Ephesians 2:21-22).

If you act upon the Word you open an avenue of access for the Holy Spirit's embrace.

The new Testament model for coming before the Lord places great emphasis on corporate worship and unity—in prayer and praise. It is not an assumption, but what God expects. Jesus prayed, *"That they all may be one; as thou, Father, art in me, and I in thee, that they also may be one in us"* (John 17:21 KJV).

This includes togetherness in worship—regardless of the church, denomination, doctrinal stance or theological position the person next to you represents. Unity in Christ means we can worship with others whether they have hands raised, head bowed, praising loudly or sitting quietly. In Jesus we are a structure joined together which becomes a temple of praise.

THE SPICE OF LIFE

You may be a person who feels awkward or ill-at-ease trying to worship in a particular style. It is good to know you don't have to imitate someone else in your praise—God responds to what you express from your heart. If the Spirit is leading you, that's all that matters.

In both the Old and New Testament, we find services with a wide variety of music and singing. Those who don't like drums in the church should take another look at Psalm 51—they praised the Lord with everything from cymbals to tambourines and dancing!

On the other hand, we can come before the Lord in

total quietness: *"Be still, and know that I am God"* (Psalm 46:10).

Variety is not just the spice of life; it is a foretaste of eternity and glory itself. Since the church is a divine organism, both variety and unity are necessary. Sadly, however, in many churches there isn't fusion, but *confusion.* It is time to relax concerning our likes and dislikes and remember Christ Himself tells us what binds the body of believers together. Jesus says: *"And I, when I am lifted up from the earth, I will draw all people to myself"* (John 12:32).

THE TEMPLE WITHIN

I have been asked, "Is it possible to live a Christian life if there is no one around you who is a believer?"

Of course it is. The apostle Paul tells us, *"Do you not know that you are God's temple and that God's Spirit dwells in you?"* (1 Corinthians 3:16). And he adds, *"Or do you not know that your body is a temple of the Holy Spirit within you,*

"IS IT POSSIBLE TO LIVE A CHRISTIAN LIFE IF THERE IS NO ONE AROUND YOU WHO IS A BELIEVER?"

which you have from God, and that you are not your own? For you were bought with a price; therefore glorify God in your body" (1 Corinthians 6:19-20).

Christianity is so personalized that you and I were

purchased one by one. When Jesus went to the cross He didn't just pay for an entity called "the church," but for individuals—one soul at a time.

While organized churches are part of God's plan for building His Kingdom, we also have the temple of the Lord dwelling within us—and it's our personal responsibility to establish a direct relationship with the Father. A Christian is someone who is a "Christ one"— an *anointed* person, after the same manner as Jesus Christ who was anointed by the Holy Spirit and went about doing good and setting free all of those who were sick or dominated by the devil. (Acts 10:38).

Yes, you can be a Christian all by yourself, but God knows the power and anointing are multiplied when we join forces. That's why we are counseled regarding, *"Not forsaking the assembling of ourselves together"* (Hebrews 10:25 KJV).

A SACRED STOREHOUSE

What a great heritage we have as believers. It began with the Old Testament saints and continues with God's Holy Spirit being available to us at this very moment.

Should the day ever come when our freedom to publicly worship is suppressed, we know that absolutely nothing—not laws, dictators nor godless tyrants—can ever stop our communion and fellowship with the Father through the Spirit. By hiding God's

Word in our heart, we have a sustaining storehouse of treasure. It's for us, our children, and our children's children.

Never neglect making time for faith-inspired, Spirit-led worship. It is a direct connection to your Heavenly Father.

MY PRAYER FOR YOU
May the same Spirit who gave power to the Son of God touch your life today. I pray your lips will be filled with continual praise, worship and adoration so you, too, can enter into the presence of the Almighty.

CHAPTER 6

THE EVIDENCE

If your awareness of the Holy Spirit's activity is limited, it is difficult to live in faith.

In Paul's letter to the believers at Rome, Paul speaks of faith as a gift, with a *"measure"* of it being given to everyone (Romans 12:3). After all, a certain amount is required to have the ability to accept the redemptive act of Jesus on the cross: *"For by grace you have been saved through faith, and this is not your own doing; it is the gift of God"* (Ephesians 2:8).

As a Christian, our faith continues to build and grow stronger as we hear more and more of the Word. The Bible tells us, *"...faith comes from what is heard, and what is heard comes through the word of Christ"* (Romans 10:17).

The only way to hear this word is through the written scriptures the Holy Spirit inspired specific individuals to write—or through the touch of the Holy

Spirit as He fellowships and communicates with us.

IN PERFECT HARMONY

The Spirit knows the Father and Son are in perfect union and Jesus would *never* put forth any word He had not heard from the Father. So the apostle Paul, when he was using the word "Christ" to refer to the Anointed One, was trying to demonstrate to the early church that the Father and the Son were absolutely in complete harmony.

To grow and develop our original amount of innate faith we must live in a manner where we feed on the Word of Christ—and be positioned to receive the gift of faith from the Holy Spirit. This "present" will be there when it is needed.

Those who live in faith, because they have experienced the love and embrace of the Holy Spirit, have a prayer life which is alive. This communication is much more than simply repeating certain words. For example, a minister who is living in this atmosphere imparts messages from the pulpit far beyond language.

WORDS FROM ABOVE

When the Holy Spirit is present and active, you may be led (as the Word foretells) to prophesy—giving a genuine message from God. You will speak the words of Jehovah, see the creative power of His words, and confirm that scripture does, indeed, have authority.

People embraced by the Holy Spirit will be living in faith to the extent that when they pray, preach or prophesy it will be far more than human utterance. They will actually speak the words given to them by the Holy Spirit. Consequently, they will see results.

IMPORTANT QUESTIONS

It is natural to expect the Spirit to speak words of instruction, make a statement or give us direction. However, at times He simply asks questions.

Two of the greatest teachers of all time—Jesus and Socrates—are known for their probing questions. (And many scholars have paralleled these lives since both died in what has been described as a martyr's death.)

IT IS NATURAL TO EXPECT THE SPIRIT TO SPEAK WORDS OF INSTRUCTION, MAKE A STATEMENT OR GIVE US DIRECTION.

Socrates (469-399 B.C.) confounded authorities in Athens because he would answer a question with a question—known today as the "Socratic method." His teachings related to how we are to live with our fellow man. Some Greek leaders thought he had a negative influence on the youth, which resulted in his trial and death.

Hundreds of years later, as Jesus walked the earth, He often taught by either posing a query or answering a question with a question. For example, on one occasion, Jesus asked His disciples, *"Who do people say that the Son of Man is?"* (Matthew 16:13).

They answered Him, *"Some say John the Baptist, but others Elijah, and still others Jeremiah or one of the prophets"* (v.14).

Rather than commenting on the reply, Jesus asked one more question: *"But who do you say that I am?"* (v.15).

Simon Peter gave an answer which has echoed through the halls of faith for over 2000 years. He replied, *"You are the Messiah, the Son of the living God"* (v.16).

Jesus responded to Peter's statement of faith by saying, *"Blessed are you, Simon son of Jonah! For flesh and blood has not revealed this to you, but my Father in heaven"* (v.17).

As the Holy Spirit deals with us, He often makes an inquiry of us. This honors Jesus since He is carrying on the same teaching method of our Lord.

THINKING WITH GOD

I remember the time in prayer when I was earnestly seeking an answer from the Lord. Distinctly, I heard the Holy Spirit ask me two questions: First, "How would you like to think God's thoughts?" Then He asked, "How would you like to think *with* God?"

Not only did I receive the answer I needed, I was

lifted to a new spiritual level and was given greater insight into heavenly matters. To this day I continue to be astounded by the precious covering of the Holy Spirit.

TOUCHING THE INVISIBLE

Any ministry that shows evidence of the Spirit in operation is providing convincing proof of His existence and activity. I am referring to people receiving a word of knowledge, being slain in the Spirit or physically healed.

I have experienced these manifestations in my ministry, as have hundreds of thousands of servants of the Lord. For example, while I do not claim to possess any special gifts, I have watched people fall under the power of the Holy Spirit when I reached out to touch them—and sometimes even *before* I laid my hands on them.

ANY MINISTRY THAT SHOWS EVIDENCE OF THE SPIRIT IN OPERATION IS PROVIDING CONVINCING PROOF OF HIS EXISTENCE AND ACTIVITY.

The term "slain" in the Spirit is difficult for some to understand, however, the term The word describes the phenomenon because when people fall under the power of God they are often so quiet it's as though they have died.

Others interpret this to mean something "old" in them has passed away so that something "new" could be born.

We earlier referred to what took place at the dedication of Solomon's temple. It is significant that when the priests came out of the Inner Sanctuary, they *"could not stand to minister because of the cloud: for the glory of the Lord had filled the house of the Lord"* (1 Kings 8:11) God's presence was so overwhelming, they fell to the ground as if dead.

GOD'S PRESENCE WAS SO OVERWHELMING, THEY FELL TO THE GROUND AS IF DEAD.

A similar reaction was experienced by John on the island of Patmos where we writes, *"I was in the spirit on the Lord's day"* (Revelation 1:10). Suddenly, someone "like a son of man" appeared (v.12) dressed in a robe reaching down to his feet. It was Jesus.

Next, as John describes the encounter: *"...his face was like the sun shining with full force. When I saw him, I fell at his feet as though dead"* (vv.16-17). He was slain by the power of God.

A LESSON BEHIND BARS

Allow me to share an incident which happened when I conducted a service in the chapel of the oldest maximum security prison west of the Mississippi River.

With me was a group of several men and women and together we set up a long table for a panel discussion regarding spiritual matters. Each of us made a short presentation, followed by a time when the inmates could come to a microphone and ask questions.

To be honest, these services were dull, lifeless and we could see virtually no impact on the prisoners who attended the chapel meetings. There was no evidence of lives being changed.

In retrospect, I realize this became a rather secular event and the Spirit had been excluded from our program.

Had I been an expert on the Holy Spirit (I'm not to this day), we would have had some specific and focused prayer time before we entered the prison gates. We should have placed our efforts before God and asked the Holy Spirit to be with us as we ministered. It would not be scheduled as a service for fielding questions (even complaints) of those incarcerated, rather a time to offer manna, spiritual food. The Holy Spirit would have been present as we honored Jesus.

Our human approach was to walk in as heros or champions for the cause of the inmates. The Lord was not being lifted up; therefore there was no manifestation of the presence of God.

"DRUNK IN THE SPIRIT"

After following the same format for two months in a row, I felt led to preach in the chapel and permission from the prison was granted. Just before the next service, I told one of the chaplains, "I want to give an invitation to personally pray with the inmates and anoint them with oil if the Lord so leads."

I'm sure they were surprised at the sudden change of style from these rather reserved Methodists, however, they responded, "Sure. That will be just fine."

Starting early in the day, I prayed for guidance and when it came time to preach in the early evening, a unique anointing washed over me as the Holy Spirit began to fill the room. When I gave the invitation, the area surrounding the platform was packed with inmates. Many were slain in the Spirit and several—as they were falling under the power of God—began to speak in a heavenly language.

It was one of those unforgettable moments when I felt the awesome power of God so forcibly I had trouble standing or focusing on things physical.

This is often referred to as being "drunk in the Spirit." The saying goes back to what occurred when the 120 came out of the Upper Room, literally staggering under the anointing of God. Peter, standing with the disciples, addressed the astonished crowd, saying, *"Men of Judea and all who live in Jerusalem, let this be known to you, and listen to what I say. Indeed, these are not drunk, as you suppose, for it is only nine o'clock in the morning. No, this is what was spoken through the prophet Joel"* (Acts 2:14-16).

Several times I almost fell off the platform and the prisoners would reach out and help me maintain my balance. That afternoon, this not only happened to me, but also to many of the inmates.

BLINKING LIGHTS!

In the prison service I laid hands on and prayed for nearly 100 individuals. At 8:30 P.M., however, the guards started blinking the lights to tell us our time was up. So I brought the service to a close.

Jesus was honored and lives were changed. Even the chaplains expressed how they were blessed and brought closer to God.

The next month we returned to the prison and once again the Lord honored His Word and I preached under the power of the Spirit. When the invitation was given, the men rushed the

WHEN THE INVITATION WAS GIVEN, THE MEN RUSHED TO THE PLATFORM.

platform and I began anointing them as fast as I could. I would barely touch them and they fell before the Lord.

Looking at my watch, I began to walk off the platform as I had done the month before, but the inmates grabbed me and brought me back to the throng of men seeking to experience the mighty power of the living God. The presence of the Holy Spirit was extremely intense and there was an awe-inspiring sense of God's *closeness* in this maximum security prison.

That evening the guards were respectful of what was happening and did not blink the lights at the normal quitting time. They allowed us to continue while the Holy Spirit was at work. I'm convinced the guards had a month to reflect on what they were seeing and the Holy Spirit softened their hearts.

Spiritually, the chains were broken and lives were set free!

"PLEASE UNDERSTAND"

Shortly after those prison services, I received an email message from a United Methodist pastor in my hometown asking me to hold a one-day revival in his church. Since we had not previously met, he gave me a brief written introduction about the church and then he expressed some detailed stipulations concerning what he expected from an evangelist.

Instead of answering his email, I decided to call him on the phone. He seemed a little hesitant to have me in his pulpit, but obviously there were members of his congregation who had heard of the powerful services we were conducting and wanted the touch of God on their own membership.

In simple terms I explained what often happens when I minister and the Holy Spirit begins to touch lives—including the fact sometimes people fall under the power of the Spirit. "Please understand," I told him, "I never go into a service with a certain outcome in mind. I just allow the Holy Spirit to have control."

With those stipulations, the pastor gave his approval. I could not blame him for being cautious. After all, many have been victimized by "users" and "abusers" of the Gospel.

A PROPHETIC WORD

My wife and I arrived at the church and ministered first at the early worship service which was quite formal. I was asked to wear my robe and vestments. After the choir sang and our minister of music, Cliff Wagner, presented a special song, I gave the message God had placed on my heart.

THE HOLY SPIRIT IS AN EFFECTIVE PREACHER—EVEN WHEN HE SPEAKS THROUGH WEAK, CLAY VESSELS.

While I do not claim to be a "prince of the pulpit," the Holy Spirit is an effective preacher—even when He speaks through weak, clay vessels.

PAUL COLLINS

When I gave the invitation a mother responded and came to the front with her son who was about 12 years old. The young lad was kneeling at the communion rail and the pastor was seated on the front pew.

Under the direction of the Holy Spirit, a prophetic word came from my lips concerning the boy. It spoke of the ministry he would one day have.

THE CONFIRMATION

The following Sunday the pastor told his congregation, "When I heard Paul Collins prophesy over the boy, I knew he was hearing from the Holy Spirit because the Spirit has been telling me the same thing."

The prophetic word had resonated in his heart too, but he had been reluctant to share it with anyone else. Then, when he heard it spoken by a stranger under the anointing of God, the pastor received a confirmation of what he had been hearing.

It was the Spirit Himself who provided victory. I did not realize it at the time, but something broke in the heavens once the pastor believed. An outstanding man of God became more empowered because of the ministry of the Spirit.

That same morning a woman was healed of a physical ailment which had plagued her for years—and her husband received healing for a condition resulting from a job-related accident.

100

In that United Methodist church, the Holy Spirit honored Jesus and He provided victory.

TOTAL DEPENDANCE

I admit I embrace the Holy Spirit because I love Him and need His presence, security, assurance and the comfort of His all-encompassing love.

Just like a minor child living at home who is still dependent on parents, that's how I feel about the Holy Spirit. Being totally reliant on Him, I need everything He has—and pray it will never change.

MY PRAYER FOR YOU
*May the power of the Spirit
become vibrant and alive within you—
confirming the Word, strengthening your faith,
guiding your walk and giving evidence of
His supernatural work on earth.*

CHAPTER 7

WALKING THE NEIGHBORHOOD

In the summer of 1979, two years after the Holy Spirit became real and alive in my life, my wife and I had returned to Missouri after working with a ministry in Wichita, Kansas. She was now on the staff of a nursing home and I was unemployed.

During those days I found myself taking long, introspective walks through the neighborhood where we were living. At the time, I just wanted to get out of the house and try to hear from God.

I've lost count of the hours I strolled through the streets, or how many miles I journeyed, but those days had a profound impact on my life.

As I walked, I thought about my present situation. Why was it nothing seemed to be working for me? Why were we struggling financially?

On some of those walks I would pray in a heavenly language, expecting the Holy Spirit to speak to me—to give me a revelation explaining why I was in such a predicament, and when I would be able to escape my "valley of troubles."

I wasn't hearing or seeing any hope on the horizon. Even though I grew up in a humble area "on the wrong side of the tracks," I had never known a time such as this when we were so hard pressed.

I really needed to hear from God. Where was the Holy Spirit? I had felt His touch before; why not now?

A TOUCH ON MY SHOULDER

My mind flashed back to the Wednesday night prayer meetings at the ministry in Kansas where we spent a great amount of time on our knees in the chapel. We would begin and close the mid-week gathering by kneeling by our chairs in fervent prayer.

On one such occasion, when I was trying to pray through my doubts concerning the validity of the ministry in which we were involved, I felt a touch on my left shoulder. It was so real I automatically looked behind me to see who it was.

There was no one there, so I knew immediately I had experienced a touch from God. He was reassuring me I was not alone.

The message flooded my mind that the Lord wasn't way out in the distance ahead of me, but right there *beside* me. The Holy Spirit was comforting me, saying, "You go ahead with your efforts, I am behind you all the way."

THE SIGNS OF "MY" TIMES

While taking one of my daily strolls, I desperately wanted to experience that heavenly touch again. I needed the assurance He was indeed standing with me on my journey.

The touch didn't come.

This "valley" caused me to spend hours trying to interpret what I would call the signs of the times, more appropriately the signs of *my* times. Whether walking or at home, I constantly was attempting to make sense of any signal, no matter how insignificant, which could provide direction for my future. I was continually looking and listening, crying out to hear from God. Very small things would crop up and I would be trying to interpret them in terms of some spiritual message the Lord was preparing to give me.

I WAS CONTINUALLY LOOKING AND LISTENING, CRYING OUT TO HEAR FROM GOD.

Life seemed to reach a dead end. Ministry doors remained closed and when I would apply for secular employment I was told either, "You're over-qualified" because of my educational background, or "You don't have enough experience in this field."

Also, being in my 40's and a minister of the Gospel, employers sensed the moment I had an opportunity to return to formal ministry I would be gone.

For the first time in my life I became aware of my total dependance on God.

TWO VOICES

As I reflect back, I know without any shadow of doubt God was behind me all the way. However, there were some issues I needed to walk through in order to have a more complete understanding of the way the Holy Spirit actually operates within a person who is supposed to be Spirit-filled and Spirit-led.

IT SEEMED THAT TWO DIFFERENT MESSAGES WERE BOMBARDING ME.

There were likely many times the Spirit *was* speaking to me, but I didn't hear Him. Why? Because I was so consumed with *self* it was blocking my ability to communicate—so caught up in the problem I really wasn't open to the solution.

It seemed that two different messages were bombarding me. In one ear, I heard the sound of hope and encouragement, in the other a dissenting voice, causing me to become mired in my problems. After

EMBRACED BY THE SPIRIT

that realization, I made a conscious effort to close my "negative ear" and listen to the voice of the Lord.

LISTENING FOR THE SPIRIT

Walking alone, I would pray audibly and at other moments silently. I learned the true meaning of Paul's admonition to "pray without ceasing"—because even though I was greeting neighbors and watching out for stray dogs, it didn't break my communication with the Lord.

During these dark days my prayer language developed to a level it had never before reached.

When you pray in tongues it is always audible. I believe "glossolalia" is a verbal expression because God wants our hearing to be impacted. Once again, *"faith comes from what is heard"* ((Romans 10:17).

You may ask, "Doesn't God hear us when we pray silently from our heart?"

Of course He does. However, *we* need to hear ourselves pray. Paul taught that the Holy Spirit would pray *through* us—therefore we need to hear what the Spirit has to say. That's why it is important to listen to Him with our physical ears.

HIGHER GROUND

I continued to question God, asking, "Why? Why are you taking me through this valley?"

I had no idea this period of isolation from work and ministry was drawing me closer to the Spirit of God and preparing me for the destiny He had planned.

"Walking the neighborhood" continued for nearly one year. Then, through an unexpected conversation with a man I had met many years earlier in seminary, the Lord miraculously began to swing wide the doors of service. I was first invited to become the interim pastor of a congregation at a rural church in a mainline Christian denomination. Soon, one more door opened and for the next three years I filled the pulpit of another small-town church.

It must have been quite a shock to that congregation to have a pastor who not only preached about the person of the Holy Spirit, but had a personal relationship with Him. It wasn't long until people were filling the pews as the power of God was manifest in the services.

Gone were the days when I was trapped in despair. Thank God, He led me to higher ground.

IS IT THE LORD?

I learned valuable lessons during my "time out" from ministry. It gave me a greater understanding of the workings and operation of the Spirit.

For example, there are moments people will hear, or receive an impression, and they believe they have heard from the Holy Spirit. In truth, since they do not recognize His voice, they could be hearing from an *unclean* spirit.

Satan does not have the characteristics of God. He is not omniscient, omnipresent, or omnipotent, but he does have "evil spirits" who imitate the *Holy* Spirit. These demons attempt to attract our spiritual ear.

Since the devil is always the imitator, God gives people the gift of discernment through the Holy Spirit. This gift is not only to perceive what a person may be thinking when they are speaking to you, or what action you should take. The basic purpose of this

BY ELIMINATING THE DISCORDANT VOICES OF UNCLEAN SPIRITS, IT IS POSSIBLE TO KNOW WHAT GOD IS DOING AND SAYING.

spiritual gift (1 Corinthians 12:10) is to recognize the spirits as to whether they are from God or Satan.

By eliminating the discordant voices of unclean spirits, it is possible to know what God is doing and saying. This gift of the Spirit will eliminate any doubt concerning the impressions we are receiving. We will know they are from the Lord.

Also, when we are certain it is the Holy Spirit we are hearing, we are able to make a valid judgment concerning what action to take or things to avoid. By recognizing the Spirit's voice, we know any thoughts we receive about people is more than mere opinion.

We're dealing with reality which has come from the Spirit of Truth.

THOUGHTS FROM ABOVE

The Holy Spirit is invisible, yet that doesn't mean He is incapable of touching us. He is the communicator and He speaks not only what He hears the Father say, but also God's *thoughts*—a point that's missed by many.

HE SPEAKS NOT ONLY WHAT HE HEARS THE FATHER SAY, BUT ALSO GOD'S THOUGHTS.

The Almighty declares, *"For my thoughts are not your thoughts, nor are your ways my ways...For as the heavens are higher than the earth, so are my ways higher than your ways and my thoughts than your thoughts"* (Isaiah 55:8-9).

His thinking far exceeds the ability of the natural mind to ascertain or to explain. Likewise, the Holy Spirit hears and knows the thoughts of God just as certainly as He knows the reflections and intents of our heart. Even greater is the fact the Spirit is able to communicate this divine information to us.

THEY ARE ONE

It is vital to understand that because the Holy Spirit is referred to as the Third Person of the Trinity, does not mean God the Father and God the Son rank above Him. There is no hierarchy which places Him in a lower position.

The Holy Spirit is a person in His own right, but just as the Father and the Son are equal in the Godhead, the three are so united they are One.

Both the Son and the Spirit know God's thoughts, but it is the Holy Spirit (not Jesus) who speaks to us.

SPIRIT-LED ANSWERS

The Spirit becomes your internal "warning system" to keep you from falling prey to those who would ensnare you. Remember, in the last days, *"...there shall arise false Christs, and false prophets, and shall show great signs and wonders; insomuch that, if it were possible, they shall deceive the very elect"* (Matthew 24:24 KJV).

The Spirit-led believer is able to see world conditions as they actually are, and how eschatology—the doctrine of "the last things"—line up with scripture as we prepare for the Second Coming.

This does not mean we will have the exact date revealed to us, but it's interesting that the one person of the Godhead whose specific assignment is to live in us, talk with us, and do everything to honor Jesus actually knows precisely when our Lord will return.

Think of it! We are very close to the one who has

the answer to the question about the end of time, the rapture (the doctrine of the "catching away" of the saints before a time of tribulation), and the Second Coming (when Jesus will return to set up His 1000 year rule upon the Earth).

As I ponder those years, my walks through the neighborhood were certainly not for physical exercise. I was in training—getting in spiritual shape for the challenges I would face in the days ahead.

MY PRAYER FOR YOU
Though you may walk through the valley of the shadow, I pray the Lord will be your Shepherd, leading you beside still waters, restoring your soul and guiding you in paths of righteousness.

CHAPTER 8

THE GIFTS IN OPERATION

In the United Methodist churches I pastored, Wednesday nights were usually dedicated to prayer. There was no special music and I didn't preach a message. With very little conversation we would go directly into sharing prayer requests and spending time calling on the Lord.

One particular evening, seated with a small group, I felt the Holy Spirit leading me to share one aspect of my spiritual experience I rarely discussed openly—since it could so easily be misunderstood.

Hesitantly, I told those present what I mentioned earlier in this book—how that at the start of my ministry, and many times since, I felt a tingling sensation in my hands. I explained, "When this occurs, it is like a fire in the palms of my hands which extends out past my fingers."

While talking, I motioned with my hands toward the group of more-than-interested listeners.

As I continued sharing, I noticed a woman in her late 60's touch the small of her back.

At the end of the prayer meeting, this same woman raised her hand and asked to speak. "Brother Paul," she began, "right at the time you stretched out your hands, I felt the power of God touch my back. At first I felt a warm heat, then suddenly the pain which I have experienced for many years was gone!"

She was rejoicing and excited—as was every person present!

PASSIONATE PRAYER

The Holy Spirit's touch and healing of this lady ushered in an entirely new dimension for the Wednesday night prayer meetings. The praying in our church became much more earnest and directed as we audibly entreated Almighty God on behalf of many concerns.

One elderly gentleman (a former missionary) would pray so passionately that I came to understand how the Spirit prays with great "moaning from the deep."

We were still gathering as we had before, but now we knew God wanted to draw closer to us and even touch our bodies. The Holy Spirit descended on those meetings and we could feel His mighty presence.

It became the "norm" for me to lay hands on each person and pray. As the Spirit continued to guide and teach us, we were learning about His tender embrace.

A WORD FROM ABOVE

It was in this same church, for the first time the Lord gave me a "word of knowledge" (when the Holy Spirit tells you something specific you did not and *could not* have otherwise known—1 Corinthians 12:8).

In the main sanctuary, a woman was kneeling at the communion rail. As I laid hands on her and started to pray, unexpected words fell out of my mouth. Quietly, I told her, "The Lord has impressed upon me there is a small child in your extended family who has a back

AS I LAID HANDS ON HER AND STARTED TO PRAY, UNEXPECTED WORDS FELL OUT OF MY MOUTH.

problem that is going to require multiple surgeries to correct. In the days to come you will be babysitting while the parents are out of town. As you pick up the child, your hands will touch the youngster's back and she will be healed."

Although I hesitated to give this prophetic word, fearing people would think it was *me* speaking instead of God, I felt *compelled* to share what the Spirit had spoken to me.

A few days after praying with this woman, I learned what took place. She *did* have a small granddaughter whose spine was not aligned properly. Then one morning, just as the Spirit had revealed, she picked up the child, and as she touched the little girl's back, she realized her granddaughter had been healed. Immediately, she called the parents and gave them the wonderful news.

When the child was taken back to the orthopedic surgeon, all he could say was, "I don't know what happened, but her back is straight."

"I DON'T KNOW WHAT HAPPENED, BUT HER BACK IS STRAIGHT."

The mother knew what the grandmother had told her and replied, "Well, we know what happened!"

The next Sunday the entire family attended church to give testimony to God's miraculous healing power. Months later, when I asked the grandmother how the child was doing, she exclaimed, "Oh, Pastor," she is tall and straight and so beautiful! Praise the Lord!"

THE PRAYER OF FAITH

In that church, God continued to demonstrate His mighty works.

One Sunday morning, after I had finished teaching a class for adults, a leading layman in our community came up to me and told me in a hushed tone, "Pastor

Collins, I would like to come to the altar at the close of the service and have you pray for me."

I could tell this gentleman, who was greatly respected by his peers, was seriously troubled. Never before had I remembered seeing him at the altar or communion rail for prayer, so I knew this was an important matter.

Just before I laid my hands on him for prayer, he shared with me there was a spot on his lung which was suspect and further testing would take place the next day.

As I began to call on God, several others in the congregation came to the front to pray along with me. Their hearts were heavy.

We were putting into practice what the Bible teaches: *"Are any among you suffering? They should pray. Are any cheerful? They should sing songs of praise. Are any among you sick? They should call for the elders of the church and have them pray over them, anointing them with oil in the name of the Lord. The prayer of faith will save the sick, and the Lord will raise them up; and anyone who has committed sins will be forgiven. Therefore confess your sins to one another, so that you may be healed. The prayer of the righteous is powerful and effective"* (James 5:13-16).

"HANGING IN THE BALANCE"

It wasn't the Methodist robes and stole which I

117

wore that day, or the office of authority I held, which gave me the confidence I needed as I anointed this leader of the congregation with oil. I could only rely on the precious promises of God's Word.

I had a sense that if the Lord would do something for this man, the rest of the congregation would see and believe. It was as though all the work the Holy Spirit had been doing in my life and in this church was hanging in the balance of this prayer.

I raised my right hand toward heaven and asked the Spirit to help me pray for this individual. Then I laid hands on him, anointing him with oil and prayed audibly. The others kneeling with us, prayed silently.

The next day the man went to the doctor; but the news was not what we had prayed for. He, indeed, did have a spot on his lung.

"WAIT JUST ONE MINUTE"

Did our prayers fail? Did God not hear and answer?

I know the Father is faithful to His Word and Jesus tells us, *"Whatever you ask for in prayer with faith, you will receive"* (Matthew 21:22).

The surgery time was scheduled to have a large portion of his lung removed in an attempt to save his life from cancer. He was expected to live for no more than three months.

After one of the doctors on the surgical team left the room, my wife and I, with the family, gathered around his bed for prayer.

As I prepared to read a few verses of scripture, my wife said, "Wait just one minute"—and she headed for the door.

"Where are you going?" I wanted to know.

"I'm going to get that doctor and have him with us as we pray."

She returned with the surgeon in tow and I made some rather feeble remarks to the effect, "Doctor, you see my wife is a Christian and we believe in prayer."

"I'M GOING TO GET THAT DOCTOR AND HAVE HIM WITH US AS WE PRAY."

He surprised us when he responded, "Well, I'm a Christian and I believe in prayer, too." He stayed with us as we prepared to hear the scripture and join hands to pray.

IT WASN'T OVER

In the hospital room I shared the story of Virginia's healing several years earlier and how God had honored our reading of the 91st Psalm. I told those gathered around the bed that I believed it was a faith-building chapter. When I read the verses this time, I was acutely aware of the presence of the Holy Spirit.

For the next several days, I visited the patient in intensive care and continued to pray the prayer of faith.

How the congregation and I rejoiced when he was discharged from the hospital much earlier than expected!

Here's the amazing part. The gentleman's life was not over in the next 90 days. No. He lived twelve more years and, praise God, did not die of cancer.

"SPIRITUAL" THINKING

I've heard skeptics say, "Healing is all in the mind. If you think positive thoughts, you will feel better."

Without doubt, there is a connection between how we think and physical health, but scripture tells us that a spiritual transformation must take place in our mind. As Paul declares, *"Do not be conformed to this world, but be transformed by the renewing of your minds, so that you may discern what is the will of God—what is good and acceptable and perfect"* (Romans 12:2).

It's not about positive thinking, rather *spiritual* thinking. The Bible says, *"You were taught to put away your former way of life, your old self, corrupt and deluded by its lusts, and to be renewed in the spirit of your minds, and to clothe yourselves with the new self, created according to the likeness of God in true righteousness and holiness"* (Ephesians 4:22-24).

Just as God raised Jesus from the dead, He wants to give us healing, not sickness, and life, not death—a renewed mind and a new self!

EXCRUCIATING PAIN

Experiences such as these caused me to dig deep into the Word regarding God's desire that His children live in health. At the same time, my relationship with the Holy Spirit was growing closer day by day.

Did this give me personal immunity from physical problems? Not at all. I vividly remember the time I began to suffer with what are called "cluster headaches." They gave me excruciating pain beyond description. At

DID THIS GIVE ME PERSONAL IMMUNITY FROM PHYSICAL PROBLEMS?

one point I thought they should put a revolving door on the emergency room of the hospital for the times I sought immediate relief.

To be honest, I didn't understand how God could answer when I laid hands on someone for healing, yet, He didn't seem to hear the cries for relief from my own anguish.

There was one period when the headaches subsided for several months, then, without warning, I felt that "old familiar feeling" start with a cluster of pain on the left side of my head, behind my left ear. It then began to move upward.

The pain came on quickly, as if an old, unwelcome friend was returning. I believe it was the "flesh" side of me expressing itself—yet, at the same time, I was

121

trying to call on God. It was a battle I seemed to lose because the cluster headaches persisted week after week.

Once again, they subsided for a long period, only to resurface. This time, I realized there was more to this than simply a physical problem. Without question, because of the direction God was leading in our ministry, Satan was out to silence me.

Immediately, I began to rebuke the spirit of the enemy. I took the welcome mat away from him and replaced it with one for the Holy Spirit.

THE POWER OF AGREEMENT

"PAUL, I'M GOING TO PRAY THAT YOU'LL NEVER HAVE THOSE HEADACHES AGAIN."

One day, in a country church where I was ministering, a young farmer walked up to me and boldly announced, "Paul, I'm going to pray that you'll never have those headaches again."

Eagerly, I accepted the sincere offer of prayer from this man who had very little formal education and no theological training—but with pure faith believed God was still in the healing business. Together we agreed in prayer.

This took place many years ago and, thank God, the headaches have not even *attempted* to return.

There is power in agreement. Jesus declared, *"Again, truly I tell you, if two of you agree on earth about anything you ask, it will be done for you by my Father in heaven. For where two or three are gathered in my name, I am there among them"* (Matthew 18:19-20).

Believe *together* and the problems in your life—health, finances, relationships, work and family— *will* change for the better!

YOUR POWER TO CHOOSE

I meet many Christians who use the excuse of "It must be God's will," for their physical infirmity. To me this is a spiritual "cop out."

The Lord may allow certain things to happen, yet it is not His perfect will. Read the story of Job in the Old Testament and you will discover his trials were not caused by Jehovah. Instead, God *allowed* Satan to test this blameless, upright man (Job 2:1-10).

Much of the sickness we see today is the direct result of the fact we are free moral agents, God has given us the power to choose—and we often make foolish choices. For example, why should we blame the Lord for allowing our heart to give out if we are gluttons and eat the wrong food? Or why should we expect God to heal us of liver failure if we are a habitual drinker?

The Lord has not only given us a free will, but also

the intelligence to know the difference between right and wrong choices.

Remember this, God loves His children and desires to see them physically well. However, He doesn't force us to live a certain way; He asks us to choose obedience. There is always an "if" involved. For example, God told the children of Israel, *"If you heed these ordinances, by diligently observing them, the Lord your God will maintain with you the covenant loyalty that he swore to your ancestors...the Lord will turn away from you every illness; all the dread diseases of Egypt that you experienced, he will not inflict on you"* (Deuteronomy 7:12,15).

If we faithfully do our part, God will do His!

BEYOND ARGUMENT

TO ME, THE DEBATE OF WHETHER SIGNS, WONDERS AND MIRACLES ARE FOR THE CHURCH TODAY HAS LONG BEEN SETTLED.

To me, the debate of whether signs, wonders and miracles are for the church today has long been settled. When Jesus said, *"...these signs will accompany those who believe"* (Mark 16:17), He was not only talking to His disciples, but to you and me.

Millions and millions can testify to the fact they have personally experienced the

124

gifts of the Spirit. The same presence of God which was real in the time of Paul the Apostle, is alive and present at this moment.

There is no place in the Bible which records the cessation of the activities of the Holy Ghost. Besides, when the Spirit embraces, you *know* what has happened—and the person with an experience is never at the mercy of the person with an argument.

The gifts of the Spirit, as recorded by Paul the Apostle to the believers at Corinth, stand as a record of a man who personally knew what God desired for the church. His words are also for you:

"Now concerning spiritual gifts, brothers and sisters, I do not want you to be uninformed. You know that when you were pagans, you were enticed and led astray to idols that could not speak. Therefore I want you to understand that no one speaking by the Spirit of God ever says 'Let Jesus be cursed!' and no one can say 'Jesus is Lord' except by the Holy Spirit.

Now there are varieties of gifts, but the same Spirit; and there are varieties of services, but the same Lord; and there are varieties of activities, but it is the same God who activates all of them in everyone. To each is given the manifestation of the Spirit for the common good.

To one is given through the Spirit the utterance of wisdom, and to another the utterance of knowledge according to the same Spirit, to another faith by the same Spirit, to another gifts of healing by the one Spirit, to another the working of miracles, to another prophecy, to another the discernment of spirits, to another various kinds of tongues, to another the interpretation of tongues.

All these are activated by one and the same Spirit, who allots to each one individually just as the Spirit chooses" (1 Corinthians 12:1-11).

APPROACHING THE FATHER

The very nature of the Holy Spirit is that He is fully God. Second, He is God relating to us in a way we, as human beings, can truly understand. As flesh and bones, we cannot stand in the presence of God. It is only by encountering the Holy Spirit we can experience God and not be destroyed by His awesome power.

There are numerous instances in the Old Testament which tell us we cannot approach the fullness of Father God directly. For example, when Adam and Eve lost their covering as a result of disobedience, they could no longer approach the fullness of God (Genesis 2).

Even Moses could not come near the burning bush without taking his shoes off because the area surrounding it was holy ground. Later when Moses desired to see the glory of God, he said, *"Show me your glory, I pray"* (Exodus 33:18).

Here is God's response: *"I will make all my goodness pass before you, and will proclaim before you the name, 'The Lord'; and I will be gracious to whom I will be gracious, and will show mercy to whom I will show mercy. But...you cannot see my face; for no one can see me and live"* (Exodus 33:19-20).

The Lord continued, *"See, there is a place by me where you shall stand on the rock; and while my glory passes by I will put you in a cleft of the rock, and I will cover you with my hand, until I have passed by; then I will take away my hand, and you shall see my back; but my face shall not be seen"* (vv.21-23).

IT IS ONLY THROUGH THE SPIRIT WE CAN APPROACH THE FATHER.

In reading the New Testament, I find it fascinating that when God came close to Jesus on earth, He did not come as Almighty God—because the human body is not able to stand in the glory of the Father. Jesus was robed in flesh, so God came near Him through the Holy Spirit and alighted on Him as a dove (John 1:32).

It is only through the Spirit we can approach the Father.

HONORING CHRIST
My experience with the Holy Spirit has been that

what He does is either for the purpose of honoring Jesus—or in *response* to someone honoring Christ. It is never to glorify man.

Many who visit a service where the presence of the Lord is real and actually "feel" the anointing of the Spirit, wonder, "Why is the Holy Spirit moving in such a fashion?"

The answer: Jesus is being honored—and the Spirit suddenly is present.

If you are a participant in a worship service, study group, prayer meeting or gathering of believers, and the supernatural happens, the only way to know it is of God is to *test* whether the Holy Spirit is the one doing the work. Is Christ truly being glorified?

Scripture gives this warning: *"Beloved, do not believe every spirit, but test the spirits to see whether they are from God; because many false prophets have gone out into the world"* (1 John 4:1).

You will know what is of God when you have personally experienced the manifestation.

My friend, the gifts of the Spirit—wisdom, knowledge, faith, healing, miracles, prophecy, discernment, tongues and interpretation—are present in the church today for a divine purpose. Yes, they cause believers to be edified, but they are given so we may tell the world that Jesus Christ is Lord.

MY PRAYER FOR YOU

*I am praying you will open your heart
and soul to receive every good and perfect
gift from the Father. May the manifestations
of the Spirit be alive and active in you so
lives will be transformed and Christ
will receive honor and glory.*

CHAPTER 9

A FLAME
OF FIRE

The anointing was present in that rural United Methodist church. Both the fruit of the Spirit and the gifts of the Spirit were evident. Yet, I was praying for an even greater outpouring.

Most evenings in those days, following dinner, I would retreat to the bedroom and pray. These were special, blessed times I looked forward to because the Holy Spirit was always there.

In one such prayer session, the Spirit told me He was going to "change the direction of the ministry." Then He added He would use me to "raise up a new ministry."

I shared with my wife what I had heard, and we were excited with what the Lord had for the future of the ministry.

They "Circled the Globe"

Just after this time, I was lying in bed one night and experienced a most unusual vision. I saw the Holy Spirit as a flame—just as pictured in the book of Acts on the day of Pentecost—come out of the country church where we had seen the healings take place. The flame seemed to flow in an arc over the dark horizon and lighted on the silhouette of the city of Springfield, Missouri—then landed on a church building.

From there, the fire broke off into many pieces and spread out over a large expanse of territory. It seemed the flames circled the globe.

What was the Lord telling me? I opened my Bible and read once more the words of Jesus: *"And this gospel of the kingdom shall be preached in all the world for a witness unto all nations; and then shall the end come"* (Matthew 24:14 KJV).

Quite a Change!

A short while later, the telephone rang late on a Saturday night, waking me out of a deep sleep. It was my United Methodist district superintendent asking me if I would be willing to leave my present church.

"Certainly," I told him. "I'll go wherever I am needed."

He continued, "There is a church in Springfield I would like for you to consider."

"Tell me about it," I replied.

"It's called Pitts Chapel," then he added, "Pitts is a black church."

"Yes, I know."

Unsure of my reaction, the superintendent continued, "Paul, take all the time you want to pray about this."

Without hesitation, I told him, "I don't need time to consider it. The Holy Spirit told me months ago He was going to change the direction of my ministry. I call this quite a change!"

"IT'S CALLED PITTS CHAPEL," THEN HE ADDED, "PITTS IS A BLACK CHURCH."

As most people my age, I went to segregated schools and had not lived among people of another race, so this was certainly breaking new ground. I said, "Yes, I'll do it!"

He sounded relieved to have a positive response from me; I could hear it in his voice. Then he added, "There's just one more detail. The salary is not as much as where you are now."

"That's okay," I answered. "I'm not doing this for the money."

So I became the pastor of an African-American United Methodist Church.

SINGING! SHOUTING!

From my first Sunday in the new pulpit, I knew my appointment was God-ordained. In all of my ministry I had never heard a church choir sing with such an anointing. The music director may not have known the doctrine of the Holy Spirit, but he certainly moved with divine unction.

During the service I witnessed a manifestation I had only seen once before—in a Methodist country church where I was holding a revival. A woman started shouting! This went on for several minutes before she seemed to semi-collapse and faint. She was in the choir and other singers stood over the woman and began to fan her.

The next Sunday the same thing happened to another member.

TOUCHED BY GOD'S POWER

A few weeks later, I felt led to invite those who wanted to be anointed with oil and prayed for to come and stand before the altar. A woman walked to the front, and as I laid hands on her she fell to the floor under the power of God.

Evidently, this had never happened in Pitts Chapel before and the curious, concerned people came to the edge of their pews. "She's fine," I reassured the congregation, "The Holy Spirit is ministering to her."

Then her husband walked to the front and I asked

him about his need. After hearing his request, I anointed him with oil. I had to reach up to touch this tall man's forehead, then, as I barely laid my hand on him, down he went! He, too, was slain in the Spirit.

The Holy Spirit increased my willingness to respond to His leading. The people would line up for prayer and we witnessed many healings. It was not uncommon for a

IT WAS NOT UNCOMMON FOR A SERVICE TO BEGIN AT 11 A.M. AND CONTINUE UNTIL ALMOST 2:30 P.M.

service to begin at 11:00 A.M. and continue until almost 2:30 P.M.

"ANOINTED" OIL

Just before the 40 days of Lent, some of the women in our church fasted and prayed for God to bless the anointing oil. We stored it in a clear vase on the communion table that sat on the rather elevated platform of the church—which was very formal in its design.

As we began using this "anointed" oil, God honored the prayers of those who had fasted and called upon Him. Miracles were happening service after service.

At the end of Lent, a minister from a Nazarene church in a neighboring community, hearing what was taking place, came and asked for some of the oil.

135

"There is a layman in my church," he confided, "who has been diagnosed with colon cancer. The operation is set for Monday morning and I want to pray for him in our church next Sunday."

When the man came forward at the close of the morning service, the Nazarene preacher anointed him with this "blessed" oil and prayed for his healing.

"SIR, WHATEVER WAS THERE LAST WEEK IS NOT PRESENT THIS WEEK. YOU DON'T NEED SURGERY!"

At the hospital the following morning, the gentleman was prepped for surgery and the doctors took one last scan. A short while later, they rolled him back to his room and a physician walked in and announced, "Sir, whatever was there last week is not present this week. You don't need surgery!"

Not long after his release, I received a phone call from the man. He said, "Pastor, you don't know me, but I would like to come with my family to your church next Sunday and testify."

He walked in with his family—and for the first time I saw a complete row of white faces in Pitts Chapel! We all rejoiced as he gave God the glory for his miraculous healing.

BEYOND EXPLANATION

Over time, the oil had dwindled down to less than

three inches in the vase. One of the prayer warriors in our church, very concerned, stopped by my office and exclaimed, "Dr. Collins, what are we going to do? We're about to run out—there won't be any left when it's time to fast and pray and bless more oil."

People had been taking small amounts of oil with them to pray for others. Eight or nine vials had been mailed to England.

I thought about it and told the woman, "Well, maybe we can just find a bigger container and pour in a large amount of oil. If several of us put our hands in it one at a time, we can pray and bless it that way."

Meanwhile, one afternoon our associate pastor was in the sanctuary of the church walking back and forth in front of the rather high platform area. Suddenly, as he told me, "I looked up and saw the oil spraying up on the sides of the vase. It was refilling itself."

Please understand, nothing like this had ever happened before or since in our ministry. I can't explain it, and am only reporting what actually took place.

It was reminiscent of the Old Testament story of Elijah and the widow at Zarephath. Her jug had only a meager amount of oil, but it never ran dry. It provided for the woman, her son and the prophet (Kings 17:7-16).

The news of what happened at Pitts Chapel spread and people started coming from all over the region to a prayer meeting at 6:30 every evening. The nightly meetings lasted for weeks. Some visitors would walk in the side door of the church and barely come around to the end of the chancel area, next to the communion rail, before falling down under the power of God—with no one touching them.

Others would try to walk up the steps to the communion table, and they would fall prostrate before the Lord. It was a supernatural happening.

This unusual manifestation let me know the precious Holy Spirit, as part of the Godhead, is actively engaged in our world. We were being embraced and "hugged" by the Spirit big time!

Not only were people healed and delivered from bondage, relationships were restored and circumstances changed. People turned their eyes on Jesus.

What Was Next?

The Lord was moving in unusual ways, yet in the back of my mind I kept thinking about the vision I had received prior to coming to Pitts Chapel. Yes, the flame of the Spirit had certainly been ignited in this beautiful congregation, but what about the picture God gave me of the fire breaking off into many pieces and spreading out over a large expanse?

Was it because the choir from this church was in great demand and ministered to a wide variety of churches and events? Is this what the Lord had in mind? Oh, it was wonderful, yet I felt He had something even greater in store.

I never forgot Him saying, He would "raise up a new ministry." What would it be?

"I Redeem the Time"

During these days I had acquired the habit of going to bed early so I could spend time with the Lord in prayer. One night, as I was communing with my Heavenly Father, He interrupted me. I clearly remember saying the word "praise," when suddenly the Holy Spirit spoke something to me which seemed totally unrelated. He said, "Don't worry about your age—I redeem the time."

The Spirit read my mind! He knew I was concerned with what I would do when I reached retirement. I couldn't imagine not preaching, but where would I minister? What would I do?

"Don't Worry About Your Age —I Redeem the Time."

I thought about the words of Paul to the believers at Colosse: *"Conduct yourselves wisely toward outsiders, making the most of the time"* (Colossians 4:5).

I wondered, if the Bible tells us *we* are to redeem the time, why would the Holy Spirit tell me, "*I* redeem the time"?

Then I realized it was because of a partnership with God in Christ through the Holy Spirit, He would enable me to conduct myself "wisely" to those I was about to meet.

What was I hearing? And why was He telling me my age didn't matter?"

As I continued to pray, the Spirit added these words: "In times past I have sifted you as sand and have pressed you down into a firm foundation—upon which I will raise up a new ministry."

HIS PURPOSE FOR YOU

One of my favorite passages in the Bible says: *"We know that all things work together for good for those who love God, who are called according to his purpose"* (Romans 8:28).

I realized I wasn't in God's service to please myself, but was called according to *His* purpose. The Holy Spirit had a divine direction for my future and was about to reveal it to me.

You see, God does not come down off His throne, walk into your living room, sit down next you on the couch and say, "Here is your calling."

Instead, the Holy Spirit, who is God, comes inside you and sits in the throne room of your heart. He says, "Here is my purpose for you."

When you read the next verse in Romans, you learn *why* all things work together for good: *"For those whom he foreknew he also predestined to be conformed to the image of his Son"* (vs.29).

YOUR "SCHOOL OF INSTRUCTION"

God, the inventor of time, knew you before you came into this world. Perhaps you are beginning to comprehend what the Holy Spirit is trying to say to you about your identity—to be conformed to the image of the Son. Keep reading and you will find the purpose: *"in order that he* (Jesus) *might be the firstborn within a large family"* (v.29).

I came to the realization my identity and mission in life could never be fulfilled unless I was totally conformed to Jesus.

THE FLAME OF FIRE HAD BEEN IGNITED. WHERE WOULD IT LEAD?

The Son of God walked this earth ministering to the hurting, casting out devils and praying the prayer of faith for those with infirmities. Since this is what Jesus did, how could I have any other purpose?

The flame of fire had been ignited. Where would it lead?

In the last section of this book you will read the story of Acts Ministry—a worldwide outreach for which the Lord had spent years grooming and developing me. Everything God had allowed to happen was a school of instruction for His ultimate calling on my life.

For what special purpose is the Holy Spirit preparing you?

MY PRAYER FOR YOU
I pray the fire of the precious Holy
Spirit will fall on you today. May He give you
peace in your heart and direction for your
future. Most of all, I pray your life will be
conformed to the image of God's Son.

CHAPTER 10

STEP OUTSIDE THE BOX

What a marvelous adventure the Holy Spirit has allowed me to experience—and it still continues.

More than once, however, my mind reverts to the years the Lord was attempting to capture my attention regarding having the gifts of the Spirit operating in my life. Specifically, I think about the healing of Virginia Shortle in St. Joseph, Missouri. Why did it take me so long after that miracle to begin actively laying hands on the sick according to James 5:14?

In the summer of 1998, the phone rang at our home in Springfield. "Is this Paul Collins," the caller asked.

"Yes it is. Who am I speaking with?" I inquired.

"This is Jerry Shortle, my wife, Virginia, and I are in town and we would sure like to see you," Jerry said.

My heart took a leap and I was thrilled beyond words. It had been 35 years since I had seen this couple and now they were at a hotel just a few blocks from our home.

A SPECIAL BOOK

My mind was working overtime, flooded with memories, as their car pulled into the drive. I hurried to embrace these wonderful people.

As we talked in our living room, Virginia showed us an old, hardcover Bible I had presented to her when I pastored Hyde Park Methodist Church. "This is special to me and I've even had it rebound," she told me.

Then Virginia handed me the Bible and asked me to write something on the inside front cover. "You are supposed to sign a book when you give it to someone," she commented—something I overlooked three decades earlier.

I felt deeply honored she had kept the Bible. What I wrote could never express the love I have for the Shortles.

After a few hours of wonderful reminiscing, I told the couple about a major event we were planning for Acts Ministry, and asked if they could possibly attend.

Jerry and Virginia responded enthusiastically and returned to attend *ACTSfest*—a Christian variety production planned by Cliff Wagner, our minister of music. Cliff (who has now gone on to be with the Lord) was also the master of ceremonies for a major music show in Branson, Missouri.

A VICTORY CELEBRATION

ACTSfest, featuring many great Christian entertainers, played to two full houses on Saturday afternoon and evening in a 1,100-seat venue in Springfield, Missouri.

The next day, however, would be even more special for Jerry, Virginia and myself.

The Acts Ministry family of faith gathered for our regular, monthly "Holy Spirit Victory Celebration and Healing Service." It is often referred to as simply "Second Sunday" because that is when this special time of praise, worship and ministry is scheduled.

FROM THE MOMENT THE SERVICE BEGAN, I FELT AN UNUSUAL ANOINTING OF THE HOLY SPIRIT FALL ACROSS THE CONGREGATION.

"WITH LONG LIFE"

From the moment the service began, I felt an unusual anointing of the Holy Spirit fall across the congregation. Then, just before sharing the Word, we took time for testimonies and I asked Jerry and Virginia to come to the platform—but she was too shy.

Jerry began to tell the story of Virginia's healing from cancer. It was a joyful, spiritual and emotional presentation. He was not quite finished when Virginia stood up, turned to face the congregation and continued the testimony.

In moving terms, she told about her deliverance from the ravage of cancer which was supposed to have taken her life so many years before. She also shared how I had read Psalm 91 to her just before she went under the surgeon's knife.

The chapter ended with the words: *"He shall call upon me, and I will answer him: I will be with him in trouble; I will deliver him, and honor him. With long life will I satisfy him, and show him my salvation"* (vv.15-16).

Here it was—35 years later. Not only had the Lord answered in a time of trouble, but had given her a long, satisfying life. What a mighty God we serve!

Virginia's testimony was even more poignant when she confessed, "I have told people about my healing one-on-one, but this is the first time I have ever stood before a group to speak." Then the rather private woman took on a spiritual boldness, adding, "I know I need to do this, because Jesus has done so much for me."

When I gave an invitation to pray for those who needed a touch from God, the response was a tremendous demonstration of the power of the Holy Spirit. Jesus received the glory!

THE HOLY SPIRIT CONNECTION

As you have read this book, perhaps you realize for the first time that the Holy Spirit is not a concept of the mind, but a person as real as God and Jesus. He talks, travels, listens, gives instructions and comforts. In fact, He does these things with such regularity His activities are overlooked by most Christians.

HE TALKS, TRAVELS, LISTENS, GIVES INSTRUCTION AND COMFORTS.

I pray that as you understand His connection to the Father and the Son, you will begin an exciting journey involving faith, miracles, and other gifts of the Spirit.

Let me emphasize once more that the Holy Spirit is God. Furthermore, He is the *Spirit* of the Father and the *Spirit* of the Son.

Those who are genuinely anointed, have the indwelling presence of God and Jesus Christ. Once I came to understand this, I began to see Pentecostals and "Charismatics" from a different paradigm. No longer did I consider them so far from the mainstream they deserved to be the subject of jokes and other forms of derision. Now I saw them as people who are empowered to do the work of God—as believers who understand what it means to walk in divine wisdom, divine knowledge, divine health, and even divine abundance.

IT'S YOUR TURN

It doesn't have to be "someone else" who receives the gifts of the Spirit. What He's done for others, He is willing and ready to do for you!

THE HOLY SPIRIT IS WAITING PATIENTLY FOR THE OPPORTUNITY TO PENETRATE YOUR LIFE.

The Holy Spirit is waiting patiently for the opportunity to penetrate your life. believe it's time to recognize what He is doing—and what He *wants* to do. For example, when you invite Him in, the Spirit will increase your knowledge.

I have a background in counseling and can assure you no human psychologist or psychiatrist can give you knowledge of yourself like the Holy Spirit is able to provide.

Since no secrets can be hidden from the Spirit, He will give you "inside information"concerning yourself, your circumstances and relationships.

Psychology talks about the concept of "knowing ourselves." The truth is, the Holy Spirit is the one who will give us our identity. Because of self-imposed limits, there are many who spend years not really knowing who they truly are. Yet, when the Holy Spirit reveals to them their true identity, the limits they have placed on themselves are no longer valid.

A LID ON LIFE?

As I have shared with young people, you can put fleas in a jar with a lid on it and they will bounce up and down. They hit the lid and come back down. After this conditioning, you can take the lid off the jar and they will only jump as high as they did with the lid in place.

As sons and daughters of the Most High God, surely we can be re-conditioned to "jump out of the jar" or "get out of the box."

Many Christians confine themselves, living in a narrow space which was built for them based on a particular view. We are limited. We look down and see the floor, then look up and see the top. Even when we look left and right, there are walls keeping us inside.

EXPAND YOUR BOUNDARIES

I believe the time has come for us to step outside our confinement—to see what it looks like from the outside. The alternative is stagnation—staying in our present condition all of our lives.

If you desire to have the Holy Spirit operating in your life, start now to expand your boundaries and begin to experience a world unlike any you have ever known.

The same Spirit who embraced those who gathered in Jerusalem to receive the "promise of the Father," is ready to surround you with His love today. Will you welcome Him?

My Prayer for You
I pray as a result of reading this book,
you will spend time inviting the Holy Spirit to touch
your life as never before. May you know His voice,
follow His leading and feel His embrace today.

ABOUT ACTS MINISTRY

Early in my ministry, the Holy Spirit was speaking, yet I wasn't doing a very good job of listening! I knew He wanted me to launch a very special outreach, but I was only guessing at the details and nothing got off the ground.

It wasn't until late spring, 1993, that the entire picture was coming into focus.

For the previous two years the Lord had instructed me to shut myself away and spend every Wednesday in my study. From morning until early evening, I read the Word, prayed and learned to talk less and listen more to the Holy Spirit.

WITH EACH PASSING WEEK THE MESSAGE THAT I WAS TO FORM A UNIQUE MINISTRY BECAME CLEARER.

With each passing week the message that I was to form a unique ministry became clearer.

This wonderful time came to a close the day the Holy Spirit said, "Paul, I can speak to you on days other than Wednesdays." I knew He meant it was time to get out of my "retreat" and follow His leading.

BREAKING BARRIERS

The Lord told me He wanted a ministry which greatly resembled that of the first generation of Christians in the book of Acts. This meant a fellowship would have to be birthed ignoring denominational lines while, at the same time, respecting them for the portion of truth deposited to their hearts by the Holy Spirit.

THERE CAN BE NO SEPARATION IN THE BODY OF CHRIST AND NO BARRIERS TO FELLOWSHIP.

Likewise, believers with no organizational affiliation would have to be recognized as valid followers of Jesus and be welcomed to work with people connected to denominations and vice versa.

In addition, what was to be birthed would need to be trans-doctrinal. There could be no arguments about minor points after agreement had been met on the bedrock teachings of Christianity.

Next, we would have to be willing (even zealous) pursuers of transcultural and trans-racial connections.

There can be no separation in the Body of Christ and no barriers to fellowship.

The revelation challenged my faith.

ONE VISION—ONE MISSION

More than one person told me, "Dr. Collins, the formation of such a ministry would be impossible." Others said, "You can incorporate, but you won't be able to have unity.

The Holy Spirit had given me a very difficult assignment, yet I knew with God all things are possible.

I was at a loss concerning an appropriate name. Eventually, it seemed appropriate to use the word "Acts" since we were to resemble first century Christians as much as possible.

THE HOLY SPIRIT HAD GIVEN ME A VERY DIFFICULT ASSIGNMENT, YET I KNEW WITH GOD ALL THINGS ARE POSSIBLE.

My thought was to call the new organization, "Acts Ministries," but my wife said it should be singular—Acts Ministry." Her reasoning being, since unity was the objective, there should be *one* vision and *one* mission.

TOUCHING LIVES

First, the ministry was incorporated under the laws of the state of Missouri. Within a short time we were recognized as a non-profit 501 (c) (3). Later we received group exemption from the IRS, so the ministries accountable to Acts could give tax-deductible receipts to their contributors.

With the structure in place, and with the help of one of our founding board members, Don "Nick" Nickell, we launched a ministry which touches thousands of lives worldwide.

WE PRAISE GOD FOR THE LIVES WHICH ARE BEING CHANGED.

I began attending conventions of other organizations and joined with them to build bridges in order to promote "Unity In Christ through The Holy Spirit." This effort bore fruit and Acts Ministry has formed a strong bond with many independent Christian groups.

LITTLE IS MUCH

We rejoice at the positive growth which is reflected in those who have been mentored to receive a strong spiritual foundation and who have been ordained to fulfill their calling. Most important, we praise God for the lives which are being changed.

Today, pastors, evangelists and churches under the Acts Ministry banner are in the harvest field in many parts of the world—including the U.S., Canada, England, Mexico, Central America, South America, India, Africa and the Philippines. Many of these churches have several thousand in attendance each week.

I am astounded at how far God has brought us and I have learned not to despise small beginnings. The old adage is true "Little is much when God is in it."

NOTES

_____

_____

_____

_____

_____

_____

_____

_____

_____

_____

_____

_____

_____

_____

_____

_____

_____

To Schedule the Author
for Speaking Engagements
or to Learn More
About Acts Ministry,
Contact:

Dr. Paul Collins
Acts Ministry
P.O. Box 11084
Springfield, MO 65808

Phone: 417-866-0223
Internet: www.actsministry.org
Email: actsministry@global.net